A Retreat With Pope John XXIII

Other titles in the A Retreat With...*Series:*

A Retreat With Job and Julian of Norwich: Trusting That All Will Be Well, by Carol Luebering

A Retreat With Jessica Powers: Loving A Passionate God, by Robert F. Morneau

A Retreat With Thomas Merton: Becoming Who We Are, by Dr. Anthony T. Padovano

A Retreat With Gerard Manley Hopkins and Hildegard of Bingen: Turning Pain Into Power, by Gloria Hutchinson

A Retreat With Therese of Lisieux: Loving Our Way Into Holiness, by Elizabeth Ruth Obbard, O.D.C.

A Retreat With Francis and Clare of Assisi: Following Our Pilgrim Hearts, by Murray Bodo, O.F.M., and Susan Saint Sing

A Retreat With Francis de Sales, Jane de Chantal and Aelred of Rievaulx: Befriending Each Other in God, by Wendy M. Wright

A Retreat With Pope John XXIII

Opening the Windows to Wisdom

Alfred McBride, O. Praem.

ST. ANTHONY MESSENGER PRESS
Cincinnati, Ohio

Scripture citations are taken from the *New Revised Standard Version Bible,* copyright ©1989 by the Division of Christian Education of the National Council of the Churches of Christ in the U.S.A. and used by permission.

Excerpts from *Pope John XXIII: Shepherd of the Modern World* by Peter Hebblethwaite, copyright ©1985 by Peter Hebblethwaite, are reprinted by permission of Cassell & Company.

Excerpts from *Pope, Council and World: The Story of Vatican II* by Robert Blair Kaiser, copyright ©1963 by Robert Blair Kaiser, are reprinted by permission of Macmillan.

Excerpts from *Journal of a Soul* by Pope John XXIII, trans. Dorothy White, copyright ©1965 by Geoffrey Chapman, Ltd., are reprinted by permission of McGraw-Hill, Inc.

Excerpts from *A Pope Laughs: Stories of Pope John XXIII,* collected by Kurt Klinger, trans. Sally McDevitt Cunneen, copyright ©1964 by Holt, Rinehart & Winston, reprinted by permission of Kurt Klinger.

Excerpts from *Wit and Wisdom of Good Pope John,* collected by Henri Fesquet, trans. Salvator Attanasio, copyright ©1996 Official Catholic Directory, published by P. J. Kenedy & Sons in association with R. R. Bowker, a Reed Reference Publishing Company, New Providence, New Jersey.

Excerpts from *The Imitation of Christ: A New Reading of the 1441 Latin Autograph Manuscript* by William C. Creasy, copyright ©1989 by Mercer University Press, are reprinted by permission of Mercer University Press.

Excerpt from *Making Choices: Practical Wisdom for Everyday Moral Decisions* by Peter Kreeft, copyright ©1990 by Peter Kreeft, are reprinted by permission of Servant Publications.

Excerpts from *Saints Are People: Church History Through the Saints* by Alfred McBride, copyright ©1981 by BROWN-ROA, reprinted by permission of the publisher.

Excerpt from *Church, Ecumenism and Politics* by Cardinal Joseph Ratzinger, copyright ©1988 by Joseph Ratzinger, is reprinted by permission of The Crossroad Publishing Company; distributed in the United Kingdom and British Commonwealth by permission of St. Pauls.

Excerpt from *A Church to Believe In: Discipleship and the Dynamics of Freedom* by Avery Dulles, S.J., copyright ©1982 by Avery Dulles, is reprinted by permission of the author.

Excerpts from *Newman on Being a Christian* by Ian Kerr, copyright ©1990 by Ian Kerr, are reprinted by permission of HarperCollins Publishers Limited and the University of Notre Dame Press.

Excerpt from *The Mystery of the Temple: The Manner of God's Presence to His Creatures from Genesis to the Apocalypse* by Yves M.J. Congar, O.P., trans. Reginald F. Trevett, copyright ©1962 by The Newman Press, is reprinted by permission of Paulist Press.

Excerpts from *A Man for All Seasons* by Robert Bolt. Copyright ©1960, 1962 by Robert Bolt. Reprinted by permission of Random House, Inc.

Selections from *I Will Be Called John: A Biography of Pope John XXIII*, by Lawrence Elliott, reprinted by permission of IMG Literary, copyright © 1972 by Lawrence Elliott.

Cover illustration by Steve Erspamer, S.M.
Cover and book design by Mary Alfieri
Electronic format and pagination by Sandra L. Digman

ISBN 0-86716-258-9

Published by St. Anthony Messenger Press
Printed in the U.S.A.

Contents

Introducing A Retreat With...

Twenty years ago I made a weekend retreat at a Franciscan house on the coast of New Hampshire. The retreat director's opening talk was as lively as a long-range weather forecast. He told us how completely God loves each one of us—without benefit of lively anecdotes or fresh insights.

As the friar rambled on, my inner critic kept up a sotto voce commentary: "I've heard all this before." "Wish he'd say something new that I could chew on." "That poor man really doesn't have much to say." Ever hungry for manna yet untasted, I devalued any experience of hearing the same old thing.

After a good night's sleep, I awoke feeling as peaceful as a traveler who has at last arrived safely home. I walked across the room toward the closet. On the way I passed the sink with its small framed mirror on the wall above. Something caught my eye like an unexpected presence. I turned, saw the reflection in the mirror and said aloud, "No wonder he loves me!"

This involuntary affirmation stunned me. What or whom had I seen in the mirror? When I looked again, it was "just me," an ordinary person with a lower-than-average reservoir of self-esteem. But I knew that in the initial vision I had seen God-in-me breaking through like a sudden sunrise.

At that moment I knew what it meant to be made in the divine image. I understood right down to my size eleven feet what it meant to be loved exactly as I was. Only later did I connect this revelation with one granted to the Trappist monk-writer Thomas Merton. As he reports in *Conjectures of a Guilty Bystander*, while standing all unsuspecting on a street corner one day, he was overwhelmed by the "joy of being...a member of a race in which God Himself became incarnate.... There is no way of telling people that they are all walking around shining like the sun."

As an absentminded homemaker may leave a wedding ring on the kitchen windowsill, so I have often mislaid this precious conviction. But I have never forgotten that particular retreat. It persuaded me that the Spirit rushes in where it will. Not even a boring director or a judgmental retreatant can withstand the "violent wind" that "fills the entire house" where we dwell in expectation (see Acts 2:2).

So why deny ourselves any opportunity to come aside awhile and rest on holy ground? Why not withdraw from the daily web that keeps us muddled and wound? Wordsworth's complaint is ours as well: "The world is too much with us." There is no flu shot to protect us from infection by the skepticism of the media, the greed of commerce, the alienating influence of technology. We need retreats as the deer needs the running stream.

An Invitation

This book and its companions in the *A Retreat With...* series from St. Anthony Messenger Press are designed to meet that need. They are an invitation to choose as director some of the most powerful, appealing and wise mentors our faith tradition has to offer.

Our directors come from many countries, historical

eras and schools of spirituality. At times they are teamed to sing in close harmony (for example, Francis de Sales, Jane de Chantal and Aelred of Rievaulx on spiritual friendship). Others are paired to kindle an illuminating fire from the friction of their differing views (such as Augustine of Hippo and Mary Magdalene on human sexuality). All have been chosen because, in their humanness and their holiness, they can help us grow in self-knowledge, discernment of God's will and maturity in the Spirit.

Inviting us into relationship with these saints and holy ones are inspired authors from today's world, women and men whose creative gifts open our windows to the Spirit's flow. As a motto for the authors of our series, we have borrowed the advice of Dom Frederick Dunne to the young Thomas Merton. Upon joining the Trappist monks, Merton wanted to sacrifice his writing activities lest they interfere with his contemplative vocation. Dom Frederick wisely advised, "Keep on writing books that make people love the spiritual life."

That is our motto. Our purpose is to foster (or strengthen) friendships between readers and retreat directors—friendships that feed the soul with wisdom, past and present. Like the scribe "trained for the kingdom of heaven," each author brings forth from his or her storeroom "what is new and what is old" (Matthew 13:52).

The Format

The pattern for each *A Retreat With...* remains the same; readers of one will be in familiar territory when they move on to the next. Each book is organized as a seven-session retreat that readers may adapt to their own schedules or to the needs of a group.

Day One begins with an anecdotal introduction called "Getting to Know Our Directors." Readers are given a telling glimpse of the guides with whom they will be sharing the retreat experience. A second section, "Placing Our Directors in Context," will enable retreatants to see the guides in their own historical, geographical, cultural and spiritual settings.

Having made the human link between seeker and guide, the authors go on to "Introducing Our Retreat Theme." This section clarifies how the guide(s) are especially suited to explore the theme and how the retreatant's spirituality can be nourished by it.

After an original "Opening Prayer" to breathe life into the day's reflection, the author, speaking with and through the mentor(s), will begin to spin out the theme. While focusing on the guide(s)' own words and experience, the author may also draw on Scripture, tradition, literature, art, music, psychology or contemporary events to illuminate the path.

Each day's session is followed by reflection questions designed to challenge, affirm and guide the reader in integrating the theme into daily life. A "Closing Prayer" brings the session full circle and provides a spark of inspiration for the reader to harbor until the next session.

Days Two through Six begin with "Coming Together in the Spirit" and follow a format similar to Day One. Day Seven weaves the entire retreat together, encourages a continuation of the mentoring relationship and concludes with "Deepening Your Acquaintance," an envoi to live the theme by God's grace, the director(s)' guidance and the retreatant's discernment. A closing section of Resources serves as a larder from which readers may draw enriching books, videos, cassettes and films.

We hope readers will experience at least one of those memorable "No wonder God loves me!" moments. And we hope that they will have "talked back" to the mentors, as good friends are wont to do.

A case in point: There was once a famous preacher who always drew a capacity crowd to the cathedral. Whenever he spoke, an eccentric old woman sat in the front pew directly beneath the pulpit. She took every opportunity to mumble complaints and contradictions—just loud enough for the preacher to catch the drift that he was not as wonderful as he was reputed to be. Others seated down front glowered at the woman and tried to shush her. But she went right on needling the preacher to her heart's content.

When the old woman died, the congregation was astounded at the depth and sincerity of the preacher's grief. Asked why he was so bereft, he responded, "Now who will help me to grow?"

All of our mentors in *A Retreat With...* are worthy guides. Yet none would seek retreatants who simply said, "Where you lead, I will follow. You're the expert." In truth, our directors provide only half the retreat's content. Readers themselves will generate the other half.

As general editor for the retreat series, I pray that readers will, by their questions, comments, doubts and decision-making, fertilize the seeds our mentors have planted.

And may the Spirit of God rush in to give the growth.

Gloria Hutchinson
Series Editor
Conversion of Saint Paul, 1995

Getting to Know Our Director

'I Simply Want to Be Your Brother'
—(From 'Speech to the People of Venice')

"O my God, not little Angelo!"

That's what my sister Assunta cried out when she heard the news over her little radio in Sotto il Monte, announcing my election as pope. I, Angelo Giuseppe Roncalli, born in Sotto il Monte on November 25, 1881, one of ten children, succeeded to the Chair of Saint Peter on October 28, 1958.

I had hoped and prayed it would never happen, but realized the inevitable after the morning session that day. I left the Sistine Chapel and went to my cell. I needed to be alone. My secretary, Monsignor Loris Capovilla, brought me some lunch and ate with me in silence. I had some soup, a slice of meat, a glass of wine and an apple. I dozed for about twenty minutes and then sat at my desk to write an acceptance speech. I chose my name. "I will be called John." At four o'clock the bell summoned us back to the Sistine Chapel for the decisive eleventh ballot. At 4:50 p.m. the Cardinals elected me.

Cardinal Tisserant, dean of the college of cardinals, asked me, "Do you accept?" I replied:

> Listening to your voice,...(I tremble and am seized by fear). What I know of my poverty and smallness is enough to cover me with confusion.
>
> But seeing the sign of God's will in the votes of my brother cardinals of the Holy Roman Church, I

> accept the decision they have made; I bow my head before the cup of bitterness and my shoulders before the yoke of the cross. On the feast of Christ the King, we all sang: "The Lord is our judge, the Lord is our lawgiver, the Lord is our king: he will save us" (Isaiah 33:22).[1]

With these words, at age 77, I became pope.

One hour later I stood in the loggia of St. Peter's and looked at a crowd of 300,000 people and gave them my blessing, *urbi et orbi* —to the city and the world. In my diary, I recalled that moment:

> I remembered Jesus' warning: "Learn of me, for I am meek and humble of heart." Dazzled by the television lights, I could see nothing but an amorphous, swaying mass. I blessed Rome and the world as though I were a blind man. As I came away I thought of all the cameras and lights that from now on, at every moment, would be directed on me. And I said to myself: if you don't remain a disciple of the gentle and humble Master, you'll understand nothing even of temporal realities. Then you'll be really blind.[2]

I have been asked to tell you a little bit about myself before we start our retreat. You know I have already lived a long time, and I promise not to bore you with the details. During the retreat I will share some personal stories with you. But here let me sketch how God led me through the major developments in my life.

I was the fourth child and firstborn son of landless peasants in northern Italy. Our village in the foothills of the Alps had about a thousand inhabitants. My parents and the culture of Sotto il Monte endowed me with a strong constitution, a lively mind, a strong sense of community, family loyalty, a powerful faith, a vivid religious piety and a vigorous love for Christ and the Church. It was the best beginning and foundation I could have imagined for my life.

In 1893, just before my twelfth birthday, I entered the seminary for the diocese of Bergamo. At age fourteen I began to keep a spiritual journal, a practice that has lasted all my life. I find it has helped me in three ways: to remind me of my resolutions, to record moments of grace and insight, and to maintain a critical eye on my faults and backslidings.

I enjoyed copying inspirational maxims from various sources because they motivated me to be more fervent in my spiritual life. Lines such as the following still touch me: "The man who does not pray is like a hen or a turkey that cannot rise in the air, and if he tries to, falls down at once" (Curé of Ars). "It is natural for any man to err, but only a fool persists in his error" (Cicero). "There is no labor where one loves, or if there is, the labor itself is loved" (St. Augustine).

I won a scholarship to the Roman seminary in Piazza San Apollinare in 1901. My seminary days were interrupted by one year of military service. I was ordained on the feast of Saint Lawrence in 1904.

While in Rome, I had become good friends with Monsignor Radini Tedeschi, who became bishop of Bergamo in 1905. Tedeschi had been a chaplain for the Opera Dei Congressi, an organization designed to implement the social teachings of Pope Leo XIII. Clerical comment about earlier bishops claimed, "One did not know how to say 'yes' to anyone. Another couldn't bring himself to say 'no.' And a third hovered uncertainly between 'yes' and 'no.'"

Tedeschi had none of these problems. He chose me to be his secretary, my first assignment as a priest. I served him for ten years, and thank God I had such an extraordinary mentor. I was not only his chief assistant, but his confidante, friend and eventual biographer. I learned from him the value of visiting every parish on a regular basis. (He visited 352 in four years.) I acquired my social conscience from him, a gift that helped me with my social encyclicals.

World War I brought me back to the military where I served as a chaplain.

In 1921 I was chosen to be the national director for the Propagation of the Faith in Rome. This was the Italian equivalent of a post later held by Bishop Fulton Sheen in the United States. I traveled extensively to meet the people involved, used the press to influence public opinion, wrote materials to stimulate interest in the Church's mission efforts and increased the number of donors. In my four years there I increased the income by four hundred percent. Many have told me this is where I really learned organizational and administrative skills.

In order to advance and protect the Church's interests in a given nation, the Vatican maintains its own diplomatic corps. As an independent state, it is qualified to appoint accredited representatives to other states and to receive their ambassadors. In 1925 Pope Pius XI inducted me into the Church's diplomatic corps and assigned me as apostolic visitor to Bulgaria where I served for ten years. I was ordained an archbishop. From 1935-1944 I became apostolic visitor for Greece and Turkey, and my residence was in Istanbul. Then Pius XII named me papal nuncio to France where I served from 1944-53.

I spent twenty-eight years in diplomacy, which was not my first love. I wanted to be a pastor. Of course, Providence taught me a lot in these posts and made me familiar with and sensitive to the Balkan cultures, the Orthodox churches and the Moslem peoples. The experience did much to help me with the ecumenical movement that was developing. My years in France bred in me a love for the French people.

I was not the first choice for France. The post was offered to Archbishop Fietta, but he turned it down for health reasons. People did not know much about me. A reporter asked an official in Rome who I was. "An old fogey" was the reply. Well, I was 63 and realized I had not attended the prestigious Capranican College where the Vatican's prime diplomats were trained. I confided to a dear friend of mine, "Where horses are lacking, the donkeys trot along."

In 1953 Pius XII made me a cardinal and appointed me patriarch of Venice. It was my first real assignment as a pastor and, I thought, a satisfying conclusion to my life. Following the pattern I had learned from Bishop Radini-Tedeschi, I began parish visitations and called for a diocesan synod. I became involved in public life and did what I could to shape public opinion in accordance with the teachings of Jesus and the Church.

I enjoy pageantry and do not find it tiresome, so my installation as patriarch of Venice suited me very well. Venetians enjoy parades and many gondoliers had painted their boats for the grand occasion. I spoke to the people of Venice as directly and simply as I could:

> I want to talk to you with the greatest frankness. You have waited impatiently for me. Things have been said and written about me that greatly exaggerate my merits. I humbly introduce myself. Like every other man on earth, I come from a particular family and place. I have been blessed with good physical health and enough common sense to grasp things quickly and clearly; I also have an inclination to love people, which keeps me faithful to the law of the Gospel and respectful of my own rights and those of others. It stops me doing harm to anyone; it

encourages me to do good to all....

No doubt the great position entrusted to me exceeds all my capacities. But above all I commend to your kindness someone who simply wants to be your brother, kind, approachable, understanding.... Such is the man, such is the new citizen whom Venice has been good enough to welcome today with such festive demonstrations.[3]

Finally, as you know, I moved to the Vatican in October 1958. Three months later I announced that I would convene an ecumenical council. It would be called Vatican II.

Forgive my laundry list approach to my life story, but I think facts are helpful before getting into interpretation. I'm a lover of history and strive to get the big picture before analyzing the details. You and I will have time enough to do that together during the retreat.

Placing Our Director in Context

In my lifetime I have experienced two world wars and the Cuban Missile Crisis of October 1962. I have witnessed the downfall of Czarist Russia, the rise of Communism and Fascism and the Cold War between East and West. I have lived on a continent where the Holocaust occurred. I have seen dictators come and go and watched the economic miracle in Western Europe due to the Marshall Plan. I have also noted the emergence of the Third World and the desperate division of the rich nations of the north from the poor ones of the south, matters I addressed in *Mater et Magistra*.

In Church matters I lived through the major movements that led up to and influenced the opening of the Second Vatican Council. Many theologians were going back to the Fathers of the Church to obtain fresh insight from the sources of early Church tradition. Other theologians were trying to reconcile modern philosophy with the tradition of Thomas Aquinas. My own seminary training occurred during a revival of the teachings of Aquinas due to the impetus given to it by Pope Leo XIII.

I watched the liturgical movement grow with Pius X's restoration of Gregorian chant and his advocacy of frequent Communion. The Benedictines were doing the solid research that would give the movement substance. Pius XII advanced the papal teaching on liturgy with his encyclical, *Mediator Dei,* stating that active participation in the Mass by the laity was the greatest way to acquire the Christian spirit. The document on the liturgy at Vatican II was the fruit of these labors.

My era witnessed the emergence of modern biblical scholarship in the Church. Again, Pope Leo XIII nudged that along. He approved the opening of a biblical institute at Jerusalem under the leadership of the Dominican, Father Joseph La Grange. Much was being learned from Protestant scholarship, but there was fear that modernism, with its denial of Scripture as the word of God, might have too great an influence. Pius XII presented a balanced view on this issue with his liberating encyclical, *Divini Afflante Spiritu.*

I was especially interested in the emergence of the ecumenical movement. Because of my years in the Balkans I was first attracted to its possibilities for reunion with the Orthodox Churches, but eventually I saw its potential for unity with the Churches of the Reformation.

Another powerful aspect of the Church's mission that touched and shaped me in these years was the social teachings of the popes. I knew firsthand what poverty meant, what it did to families, how it affected the dignity of workers and what the industrial revolution had done to change the face of society. The encyclicals of Leo XIII, Pius XI and Pius XII's radio addresses on social topics were well known to me. My first assignment in Bergamo and my years in Venice brought me into direct contact with social issues and the need of the Church to be involved with them.

In my papacy I have written two social encyclicals, *Mater et Magistra* and *Pacem in Terris*. During our retreat I will allude to these as teachings that pertain to our spiritual lives and provide us with direction in our identity with the Church and its mission.

I see all of these movements as graces from the Holy Spirit moving our Church to bring hope to the world and Christ's medicine of mercy. These providential developments showed me that the Church should prefer to respond to the world with mercy rather than severity. I think we meet the needs of the present age best by showing the validity of our teachings rather than by condemnations.

These are the strands of twentieth-century history, both secular and ecclesial, that shaped my thinking and attitudes. But my soul was not confined to this century. I love history and welcome its salutary lessons. In my spirituality I have been deeply influenced by *The Imitation of Christ*, the *Little Flowers* of Saint Francis, Saint Gregory's *Moralia*, Saint Isidore of Seville's praise of Saint Fulgentius, the writings of my beloved Saint Francis de Sales and others I will call upon during this retreat.

My view of spirituality is to be at home with the wisdom of the ages, to be in communion with the saints and wise people throughout all of salvation history. Whatever identifies us with the loving and humble Christ belongs to all spirituality.

These few facts of my life that I have shared with you may help you appreciate the miracle of grace that led me to call the Second Vatican Council. Where did the actual idea come from? I was having a conversation with Cardinal Tardini. We discussed how the world was plunged into so many grave anxieties and troubles. All people of goodwill wanted peace and harmony, but conflicts were growing more acute and threats to peace multiplied. What should the Church do? Should the Body of Christ just drift with the tides of the times? Should the Church issue new warnings or become the light of the world? How could we make that light shine? At that moment grace touched me.

> Suddenly...my soul was illumined by a great idea which came precisely at that moment and which I welcomed with ineffable confidence in the divine Teacher. And there sprang to my lips a word that was solemn and committing. My voice uttered it for the first time: a Council.[4]

I draw from these impressions a profound sense of joy and hope, realizing how rich in love Jesus Christ is and how much that is given to us through his Spirit in the Church and sacraments and the witness of faithful believers. It is in this spirit I ask you to join me in our forthcoming retreat.

Notes

[1] Peter Hebblethwaite, *Pope John XXIII: Shepherd of the Modern World* (New York: Doubleday, 1984), pp. 285-286.

[2] Ibid., pp. 287-288.

[3] Ibid., pp. 237-238.

[4] Ibid., pp. 316-317.

Day One

Always Begin With Love

Introducing Our Retreat Theme

> *"Unity in necessary things, freedom in doubtful things, love in all things."*

Someone once asked me, "Do you believe, my dear Roncalli, that people improve as they grow older?"

"That depends," I replied. "People are like wines. Age improves some of them."

As I begin this seven-day retreat with you, I can tell you I wondered what the theme should be. I thought about all the gifts I have received from Jesus and the one that makes me most grateful is the virtue of wisdom. I suppose it's my age that moves me to share this gift with you. Wisdom is like a glass of good wine. Its flavor, smoothness and easy taste has resulted from a complex process.

What is wisdom? Wisdom is the capacity to see life as God sees it. It requires insight and imagination. True wisdom is always a grace from God built out of the experiences we have. In practical terms, wisdom teaches us when to speak and not to speak, when to act and not to act, to realize there is a proper time for everything. Wisdom calls us to act not just with the mind but with the heart, to behave as a whole person.

Wisdom reveals the secret of always remaining young

in heart. Wise people grow old in body, but never in spirit. Wisdom is close to the humility that shows us how to walk with kings but never lose the common touch. Jesus Christ is our best model of wisdom. He not only taught the truth, he claimed to "be" the truth. In union with him through meditation and prayer, we begin to absorb his wisdom. The richness of wisdom is too great for definition. That is why I will try to unfold its mystery over the seven days of our retreat.

Wisdom reminds me of my visit as pope to the Regina Coeli prison. I told them I had a cousin who went to jail for poaching. I said, "I have looked into your eyes. I have placed my heart alongside your hearts." Among the prisoners who came to greet me, a murderer said, "Are your words of hope meant for a sinner like me?" God gave me the wisdom simply to embrace him in silence.

Acquiring wisdom is like listening to a tree grow. It contains the leaves of love, the roots of humility, the branches of prayer, the simplicity of its color, the toughness of patience in its bark and the shade of compassion. Hold onto this picture as I unfold for you the mystery of wisdom and the complex process by which it is reached by the power of the Holy Spirit.

Opening Prayer

Jesus, living wisdom,
shorten the distance between my head and my heart.
Teach me how to think with my heart
so that all my thoughts are filled with love.
Show me that wisdom is truth tasted
in all its beauty.
Walk with me as I learn from life
how wisdom becomes my friend.

Mary, mother of Jesus and my mother,
the Church praises you as seat of wisdom.
Wise woman, pray for me
that I may receive the gift of wisdom
and the love which makes it possible.

Holy Spirit, your first gift is wisdom.
Breathe on me, breath of God,
and immerse me in this gift.
Take away my fear and fill me with love.
Show me that courage is a heart that acts,
which is a way of saying that wisdom
flows from the heart.

Retreat Session One

Show Me One Who Loves

The easiest path to wisdom is love. Desire is the key. I did not need to invent my longing for God. I needed to discover that the desire already existed within me, planted there by God. Love revealed to me the secret of wisdom.

The habit of love helped me many times. When I first became pope, I had a hard time sleeping. I felt lonely and this kept me awake. I needed more conversation and social companionship to keep me from feeling deserted.

I found that eating alone depressed me. Pius XII had maintained the custom of eating by himself. I soon invited Monsignor Capovilla to join me at the table. Then I asked the cardinals of the Curia to be my table companions, one after the other. Lastly, as the world's bishops came to Rome for their visits to report on their dioceses, they were invited to dine with me.

One day a distinguished visitor reminded me of the solitary eating habits of Pius XII. "Yes, well I value tradition as did my esteemed predecessor. But I must confess I never found any place in the Bible which suggests the pope should eat alone."

You must remember I grew up in a large family, one of ten children. I was also part of an extended family of numerous cousins, aunts and uncles. Roncallis had lived in Sotto il Monte since the fifteenth century. When we sat down to eat there were always about thirty relatives for the pasta and the polenta—a dish of maize flour. I look back on my childhood with affection but without romanticism.

> We were poor, but happy with our lot and confident in the help of Providence. There was never any bread on our table, only *polenta*; no wine for the children and young people; only at Christmas and Easter did we have a slice of home-made cake. Clothes, and shoes for going to church, had to last for years and years.... And yet when a beggar appeared at the door of our kitchen, when the children—twenty of them—were waiting for their bowl of *minestra* [vegetable soup], there was always room for him, and my mother would hasten to seat this stranger alongside us.[1]

Ever since I left home at age ten, I have read many books and learned many things that my family could not have taught me. But what I learned from my family remains the most precious and important, and it sustains and gives life to the many other things I learned later in so many years of study and teaching.

Love is first learned within the family from our parents, brothers and sisters and other relatives. When that experience is combined with a deep faith, family prayer and regular religious practice in one's parish church, then the Christian family is indeed the school of the virtues.

Yet, as you know so well, learning to love is no easy matter. I had my own painful moments, one of which involved my mother. I was twenty years old at the time.

> [T]here was an incident, which, though insignificant in itself, has made a profound and painful impression on me. My mother was rather hurt by something I said (which, I confess, might have been put more gently) rebuking her curiosity about a certain matter. She was deeply offended and said things to me which I would never have expected to hear from my mother, for whom, after God, Mary and the saints, I bear the greatest love of which my heart is capable. To hear her tell me that I am always uncivil with her, without gentleness or good manners, when I feel that I can say with all sincerity that this is not true, has hurt me too deeply; she was distressed because of me, but I was very much more distressed to see her grieving and, to put it frankly, giving way like this. After so much tender love to be told by my mother that I dislike her, and other things that I have not the heart to remember any longer—oh this was too much for the heart of a son, and of a son who feels the most profound natural affections. This gave me the most bitter sorrow, wounded the most intimate and sensitive fibres of my heart. How could I help giving way to tears? O mother, if you only knew how much I love you, and how I long to see you happy, you would not be able to contain your joy![2]

Does this surprise you? I am told people see me as a kindly old man. And perhaps I am. But the road of love is never smooth. Someone once told me that I was acting like a typical young man, loosening myself from my mother's apron strings. And she was more upset by the fact I was no longer little Angelo than with what I had said to her. That storm passed, and we had many years of deep devotion to each other.

All love has its rocky moments. That is why love must be rooted in God. Without a deep spiritual basis, love falters, fumbles and fails all too frequently. Let me share with you some meditative points which will help you build a life of love on the source of love which is God.

1. Think of the divine love that gave you existence.

Put to yourself these questions. Who am I? Where do I come from? Where am I going? All you possess, your body, mind, feelings and talents come from God. Before you were born, everything you see around you was already here. Think of it! The same sun, moon and stars, the same mountains, animals, plants and people were all abiding under the watchful eye of divine Providence. And you? You were not here. People were shopping, laughing, fighting, loving, taking vacations, complaining about bosses, having a good time, having bad times—without you. Nobody thought of you. Nobody imagined you even in their dreams because you did not exist yet.

Except God. The timeless God thought of you. With the warmth of divine love, God drew you from nothingness. The unique you is as much a creation as the cosmos itself. God gave you being, life, a soul and the faculties of your mind and spirit. God opened your eyes to the radiance that surrounds you.

God is your Lord. You are a creature. This is the most honest fact you must admit about yourself. To be frankly aware of being a creature in no sense diminishes you, because you came to be out of the generosity of divine love. You are God's love-child. It is common enough for you to brag about your existence and talents and blessings, received from God, as though they were your own. How foolish you and I can be. "What do you have that you did not receive? And if you received it, why do you boast as if it were not a gift?"[3]

Who am I? What am I doing here? Where am I going? Address these fundamental questions to yourself on a regular basis. If it is God who made you and gave you your talents and keeps you in existence, why do you think you are so necessary to the world? Your whole being resulted from God's love. Should you not admit this and praise and thank God for so wonderful a gift? I urge you to become a servant of love. Send acts of love back to God. Make many acts of love for God every day. These acts set your soul on fire and make it gentle.

What is your destiny? Heaven. Never forget you are a pilgrim on earth, a traveler to paradise. That must be your goal. In all life's inevitable disappointments, personal tragedies and bitterness recall the blessed hope of heaven. This is what all the saints did. Read their lives. Catherine of Siena and Francis de Sales and all the others. The rhythm of their hearts exclaimed, "Paradise, Paradise!"

This is the first lesson in loving, to be aware of your origin and destiny and its meaning for your earthly passage.

2. Pay attention to the reality of your soul.

You are not a stone, a plant or an animal. You are a human being endowed with incredible dignity. Modern research likes to examine our relationship with animals. I would rather concentrate on our connection to the angels. It's not hard to be aware of your body. Advertising does it for you just in case you might miss it. Sparkling teeth, bushy hair, nail care, muscle development, proper diet, shining eyes, glowing skin—the ads will raise your consciousness about this.

I am not asking you to deny the reality of your body.

That would be foolish, wrong and fatal. Your body plays an essential role in your full personal development. But don't forget your soul. Body care is fine. So is soul care. Many have teased me about my size, and I have joined them in the fun. One day, while meeting with a notably slim missionary bishop, I said—paraphrasing John the Baptist—"He must increase." Then to complete the quote, I pointed to the bishop's stout companion and concluded, "and he must decrease!"

It used to be that millionaires were the richest people. With the emergence of a global economy we now have billionaires. Your soul is worth more than all of them put together. Your soul is of infinite value because it cost the blood of God. Whether you live in a mansion with lots of rich friends as neighbors or you are homeless, sleeping on the streets of Calcutta, your soul is the most precious treasure on earth.

You cannot meditate too much on the reality and value of your soul. Your soul will survive your body at death and is destined for eternal joy. Yes, your resurrected body will rejoin your body at the second coming of Jesus, but it is your soul that provides the continuity of "you." Take care of your soul. Don't offend its dignity with sin or make it a slave of the body. The soul should command the body. This is the order of creation. This does not mean the soul should tyrannize the body, just as the body ought not to abuse the soul. God meant soul and body to work together in harmony and love according to the divine laws.

Care of the soul means growing in all the virtues, especially love. Virtues are good habits. God calls you to acquire virtues so you will not have to reinvent your life everyday. Virtue comes from a Latin word that means force and power. Virtue is to the soul what muscle is to the body. Virtues in the soul save your mind from having to worry over every challenging situation you face because virtues incline you to choose the right behavior rather than the bad.

It is in the soul that you will see most clearly that you are an image of God. Every human being is made in God's image. Yet many do not think of God or serve God. Many reject God. This thought has inspired me with compassion for souls and a burning desire to save them. If I can do nothing for them in person, I can at least pray for them. If everyone I meet is God's image, why should I not love each of them? These radiances of God all around me should motivate me to revere them, honor their glowing dignity and love them.

Poets like to speak of how sunrises and thunderstorms make them think of God. They are right. In November 1959 I received a delegation of the Catholic Women's League of Italy. My first words to them were, "Did you hear the thunder last night?[4] ...Dear God, what a storm." Hundreds of trees had been uprooted, fires were started by the lightning, roofs were blown off by the wind and numerous accidents occurred on the streets of Rome. "Believe me, my dear fellow citizens, the Pope was afraid, too. I jumped out of bed and started to pray. I chanted the Litany of the Saints and only then did my fear begin to diminish. At last I was able to get back to sleep, and this time my dreams were edifying."[5]

Indeed nature can help one think of God. But it is people who draw me to think of God. All those wonderful images of God walking around me every day. Every human being glows with the divine light. This truth must hold you and me back from ever offending any person. I ponder the humbling fact that their souls are dearer to God than my own. Pay attention to the reality of your soul.

3. Admit your sinfulness.

Now I must ask you to reflect on some issues that may not appeal to you, namely, human sinfulness and the reality of hell. The modern world values honesty and frankness. In that spirit I must be straightforward with you. I owe you the full picture of the spiritual life, so please stay with me even if you find yourself resisting this darker side of our human condition.

In every retreat I ever made, I have reflected on my sinfulness. One of my favorite parables is that of the tax collector and the Pharisee (Luke 18:9-14). Jesus addressed that parable to people who were convinced of their own righteousness and despised everyone else. Remember the story?

A Pharisee and a tax collector went to the temple area to pray. The Pharisee prayed out loud in a boastful tone that he was glad he was not like the rest of humanity—greedy, dishonest, adulterous—or even like the tax collector who was considered a public sinner. The Pharisee listed his virtues. He fasted twice a week and put ten percent of his earnings in the temple treasury. The tax collector stood back in the shadows, lowered his head and beat his breast and prayed, "O God, be merciful to me a sinner" (Luke 18:13). Jesus praised the tax collector because everyone who humbles himself will be exalted and the boastful will be humbled.

I like this story. I keep it in mind every time I enter a church or any public gathering. I am a sinner. I try to avoid arrogant words and self-important gestures. I lower my eyes and pray for humility of heart and the gift of friendliness to every person. I withdraw to the shadows of the church, beat my heart like the tax collector and repeat his prayer, "O God, be merciful to me a sinner." Then when I receive graces and consolations from God, I think of them as divine alms for a poor man. That helps me not to boast about them but be aware of my unworthiness.

I think about my vanities, all the words and witticisms prompted by a secret desire to impress others and show off my learning. I say to myself that I must think hard about my sinfulness. It is better for me to do it here rather than wait for God to do it later. "If we discerned ourselves, we would not be under judgment."[6]

Now I must speak to you of hell. One of the basic questions I put to you is, "Where am I going?" I urged you to plan on going to heaven and to keep that goal before your eyes. But, unhappily, there is another option, hell, if you decide to give up your faith in God and surrender to a life of sin. Modern society chooses not to think of hell and dismisses it as a superstitious remnant of a preliterate culture. Massive denial will not make the truth about hell disappear. So let us robustly face facts.

> The thought of hell terrifies me; I cannot bear it. It seems almost impossible to me, I cannot imagine my God being so angry with me as to drive me away, after loving me so much. Yet this is a most certain truth. If I do not fight against my pride, my arrogance and self-esteem, hell awaits me. Oh what a dreadful thought! Is it then true, O beloved Jesus, that I could no longer love you? no longer see your face? that I should be driven from you? I must hope this will never happen, but it might.... In hell the damned and the devils will keep me company, and here I cannot endure the company of a person I dislike....
>
> O my most sweet Jesus, listen to this prayer of mine. Send me, I beg you, every sort of illness in this life: confine me to my bed; reduce me to the state of a leper in the woods; load my body with all the most atrocious pains here below, and I will accept all these as penance for my sins, and I will thank you for them, but of your charity do not send me to hell, do

not deprive me of your love and of the
contemplation of you for all eternity.[7]

Tough words aren't they? May I tell you they are not severe enough. Hell is no joke. Though the love of God is the greatest motivation for living virtuously, avoidance of hell is also a powerful motivation. I hope I have given you a "shock of recognition" about a major truth of our faith.

It is said that smart people don't worry about hell. Well, Thomas More was the brightest man in England, and he worried about it. Norfolk tempted More to abandon his principles with the plea, "Can't you do what I did, and come with us, for fellowship?"[8] More replied, "And when we stand before God, and you are sent to Paradise for doing according to your conscience, and I am damned for not doing according to mine, will you come with me, for fellowship?"[9]

Jesus was quite concerned about the Judgment. His Last Judgment sermons are among the most vivid of his teachings. Remember what he had to say about the Last Judgment in Matthew 25:31-46? Notice how he combined judgment, heaven, hell and love in a seamless garment. There will be a judgment. There are only two destinies, heaven and hell. Love of people will bring us to heaven. Failure to love people will send us to hell. And one reason we love is because Jesus appears in each person we meet. In loving a person we love Christ. In failing to love, we reject Jesus. Nothing complicated in that.

Sin, judgment and hell are part of the big Christian picture. So also are virtue, judgment and heaven. Michelangelo tells it all in his splendid fresco in the Sistine Chapel where I have spent so many hours. I think you take my point. We cannot be selective about revealed truths. Faith calls us to believe in the whole picture. Admit your sinfulness. Call on God's magnificent mercy. Trust in the power of Christ's salvation.

Love makes no sense if you are committed to sinfulness. A failure to love harms people, mars our relationship with Jesus and breaks Christ's laws of love.

4. Practice friendliness.

God has blessed me with a friendly temperament. My training both at home and school taught me to treat people with courtesy and patience. In this regard I have learned a lot from my great mentor, Saint Francis de Sales, the "gentleman saint." I wish I could be like him in every way. I should be willing to endure even scorn and mockery in my goal of showing friendliness to all.

When I urge you to practice friendliness, I am fully aware of how difficult this can be. It is no simple matter to look for the good side of people and things and avoid criticism and harsh judgments. During my years in the diplomatic service, I lived at close quarters with others and I was often distressed by their failures to be friendly. I found this all especially burdensome during my years as nuncio in Paris.

> This and the considerable difference in age, mine being more full of experience and profound understanding of the human heart, often make me feel painfully out of sympathy with my entourage. Any kind of distrust or discourtesy shown to anyone, especially to the humble, poor or socially inferior, every destructive or thoughtless criticism, makes me writhe with pain. I say nothing, but my heart bleeds. These colleagues of mine are good ecclesiastics: I appreciate their excellent qualities, I am very fond of them and they deserve all my affection. And yet they cause me a lot of suffering. On certain days and in certain circumstances I am tempted to react violently. But I prefer to keep

> silence, trusting that this will be a more eloquent and effective lesson. Could this be weakness on my part? I must, I will continue to bear this cross serenely, together with the mortifying sense of my own worthlessness, and I will leave everything else to God, who sees into all hearts and shows them the refinements of his love.[10]

I think you will find, as I have, that friendliness and serenity go together. A soft answer does turn away wrath. Rough, impatient and abrupt remarks have caused too much bitterness in this world. I have heard an American expression, "Them's fightin' words!" That should be kept in mind when another saying is adopted too casually, "Sticks and stones may break my bones, but names will never hurt me." Not true. Many people have been so wounded by name calling that they never get over it. They nurse the grudge years afterwards and are weakened in their personal growth by that scar they have never taken the trouble to heal by a forgiving attitude.

I have noticed that some people are so afraid of being underestimated that they compensate with arrogant behavior and brittle self-assertion. That would be contrary to my nature. I'm a lucky man because being simple with no pretensions requires no effort from me. I praise God for this wonderful gift, and I want to preserve it and be worthy of it.

One of the purposes of friendliness is, of course, to make friends. God has blessed me with a wonderful family. They became my best friends, especially my grand-uncle Zaverio. When I was only 2 and he was 59, he, who had never married, devoted himself to me. I was his godson, and he was a father figure to me. We called him "Barba." He lived to be 88. He read widely on prayer and Church matters and was involved in the beginnings of Catholic Action in Bergamo. Over the years I have made many friends and adopted the practice of staying in touch with them. A good friendship is like a strong bridge, it must always be kept in repair. Friendship cannot be taken for granted.

In my spiritual testament to my family I stressed the importance of love. Bear with me as I quote at length from it and invite you into my family circle with so many names and connections. I guess the reason is that I can't imagine talking about love and friendship without mentioning family.

> Go on loving one another, all you Roncallis, with the new families growing up among you, and try to understand that I cannot write to all separately. Our Giuseppino was right when he said to his brother the Pope: "Here you are a prisoner *de luxe*: you cannot do all you would like to do."
>
> I like to remember the names of those among you who have most to bear: dear Maria, your good wife, bless her, and the good Rita who with her sufferings has earned paradise for herself and for you two, who have cared for her so lovingly, and our sister-in-law Caterina who always makes me think of her Giovanni and ours, who looks down at us from heaven—and all our Roncalli relations and nearest connections, like those who have "emigrated" to Milan....
>
> Be of good heart! We are in good company. I always keep by my bedside the photograph that gathers all our dead together with their names inscribed on the marble: grandfather Angelo, "*barba*" Zaverio, our revered parents, our brother Giovanni, our sisters Teresa, Ancilla, Maria and Enrica. Oh what a fine chorus of souls to await us and pray for us! I think of them constantly. To remember them in prayer gives me courage and joy, in the confident hope of joining them all again in the everlasting

> glory of heaven.
>
> I bless you all, remembering with you all the brides who have come to rejoice the Roncalli family and those who have left us to increase the happiness of new families, of different names but similar ways of thinking. Oh the children, the children, what a wealth of children and what a blessing![11]

You can see from this that family has meant a great deal to me. I know that social change has reduced the size of families, that mobility has broken up the extended family as most of us once knew it. Still the family even in its smaller form can be the home where great virtues are nourished and the practice of friendship can be stimulated.

I approach now the end of Day One of our retreat. We are addressing the theme of wisdom in general and the topic of love as a window onto wisdom. No one can be wise without love. The world is full of smart people who know a lot but lack love. It is love that turns facts and truth into the gold of wisdom. Look on everyone with the eyes of love, and you will begin to know what wisdom means.

I have shared with you some stories from my life, not so much to make you think of me, but to awaken in you your own family album and cause you to pass before the screen of your memories the stories of family, Church and friendship which have shaped your life.

My meditation points are designed to sharpen your attention to the facets of love. Think of how God's love created you. Write down the basic questions I gave you and discover how many new ways you can answer them as time marches on. Care for your souls, that part of you that so clearly resonates with the presence of God.

Acknowledge your sinfulness, not out of some morbid need to punish yourself, but because it is a fact of every human life and there is no way to appreciate Christ's salvation unless we honestly face the evil that springs up all too often in our souls. Always link the awareness of sin with Christ's medicine of mercy. Practice friendliness because it is the ordinary, everyday expression of humble love. Begin with love. There will be much more to do as we shall see.

For Reflection

Forward to the Basics

Think of your favorite Gospel scene. Picture the event in your imagination. One way to do this is to imagine you are painting the occasion, slowly, carefully, with an eye to the details such as the time of day or night, the look of the people, the face of Jesus. As it takes shape, say a brief prayer with silence between each word. Drop each word of prayer into your well of quiet. As you hear what others are saying to Jesus, ask for your turn so you can ask Christ these basic questions about yourself. Ask one question at a time. Pause and let Jesus speak to your heart. Let go of hurry and haste.

- *Who am I, dear Lord?*
- *What am I doing here?*
- *Where am I going?*

Care of the Soul

Prayer is nutrition for the soul. It gives you a desire for God. Saint Augustine says, "God wills that our desire should be exercised in prayer, that we may be able to receive what he is prepared to give."[12] Choose a quiet place and remain still. Close your eyes. Notice all the action inside. The body does not move, but your soul is like a busy harbor scene with boats coming and going, seagulls diving to get fish, somebody water-skiing. Go beneath the water and find a new depth of soul. The more you do this, the more you become aware of soul acts: imagination, memory, thoughts and the uncanny depth beyond this.

Body awareness is important.

So is soul awareness.

Soul consciousness can lead to God consciousness.

Read Psalm 139 and select a verse that strikes you.

Ride the power of the verse as it leads you inward to care for your soul.

Do this fifteen minutes a day. Increase the time as you feel drawn to do so.

Conscience Starters

Our mentor says we must become aware of our sinfulness and the bleak possibility of hell if we do not undertake lifelong conversion to Jesus. This involves the use of our conscience, which is the God-given ability to judge what is good and what is evil. The *Catechism* teaches us that guidelines for developing conscience are: natural law, the Ten Commandments, the moral teachings of Jesus, the teachings of a Spirit-guided Church and the work of the Holy Spirit.

Here is a brief prayer you can say each day to ask the Holy Spirit to give you the gift of counsel by which your conscience can be formed. The more you say this prayer, the more you sense the power of your conscience as a lifegiving gift freeing you from anything that stops you from loving God, others and self.

Come, Holy Spirit,
Convince me of my sinfulness.

Convict me of my sinfulness.
Convert me from my sinfulness.
Console me in the process.

Closing Prayer

O the love of Jesus!...Teach me your truth, the way I must go. I will cling closely to you, and I will love you, O my Jesus, I will love you with the love of Paul and of your beloved John, with the love of all your saints, the love that leads to action, the love that endures till death. Nothing can ever separate me from your love, not hunger or poverty or cold or pain, neither suffering nor death. I trust so much in the help of your grace, O Jesus!... May we all, gathering under the shadow of your adored Cross, praise your mercy forever.[13]

Notes

[1] *Familiari,* I, p. 8, quoted in *Pope John XXIII: Shepherd of the Modern World,* p. 8.

[2] *Pope John XXIII: Journal of a Soul,* trans. Dorothy White (New York: McGraw-Hill Book Company, 1964), p. 78.

[3] 1 Corinthians 4:7, *NRSV.*

[4] *A Pope Laughs: Stories of John XXIII,* collected by Kurt Klinger, trans. Sally McDevitt Cunneen (New York: Holt, Rinehart and Winston, 1964), p. 65.

[5] Ibid.

[6] 1 Corinthians 11:31, *NAB.*

[7] *Journal of a Soul,* p. 67-68.

[8] Robert Bolt, *A Man for All Seasons: A Play in Two Acts* (New York: Vintage Books, 1960), p. 77.

[9] Ibid.

[10] *Journal of a Soul,* p. 271.

[11] Ibid., pp. 336-337.
[12] Letter 130, 8, by Saint Augustine.
[13] *Journal of a Soul*, pp. 69-70.

Day Two

Simplify Your Life

Coming Together in the Spirit

"To be simple with prudence—the motto is John Chrysostom's. What a wealth of doctrine in these two phrases!"

I had scarcely been elected pope when a number of people asked me, "What titles will you bestow on your nearest relatives?" For centuries popes have had the right to award their relatives with prestigious titles. Simple people who were brothers, sisters, nieces or nephews of a newly-elected pope of humble background could quite suddenly become counts and countesses.

The pope could also reserve rooms at the Vatican for these relatives where they would live rent-free and entertain their friends. Saint Pius X, another man from peasant stock, had declined to elevate his relatives to noble status.

Now when I was asked the traditional question on this issue, I said, "Call them brothers, sisters, nephews and nieces of the pope. I believe that should be enough. It seems to me that since they wished to remain in their simple homes in Sotto il Monte, this is an excellent sign of their nobility."

Defining Our Thematic Context

Love Is the Road to Wisdom

On Day One of our retreat I established for us the theme of wisdom. I proposed that we should begin with love if we want to be wise. Jesus made it clear that love of God, others and self is the most important goal in life. I asked you to meditate on four points which are the condition of the possibility of such love: (1) Think of the divine love that gave you existence. (2) Pay attention to the reality of your soul. (3) Admit your sinfulness. (4) Practice friendliness. Now let us pray for the graces we need to continue our reflection.

Opening Prayer

Jesus, you lived so simple a life
that you had no place to lay your head.
Your simplicity was related to a firm
vision of your goal to save us from our sins.
To imitate you I should adopt the axiom,
"In all things, think of the goal."
Jesus, implant your graces of simplicity
in my mind and heart.
Mary, seat of wisdom,
you lived in Nazareth in utmost simplicity.
You didn't say a lot, but you contemplated much.
Words moved from your head to your heart
where you probed their meaning in prayer.
I am beset with modernity's complexity,
pushed and pulled by the rush of events and
the world's bonfire of vanities.
Pray for me, Mary, that I may be drawn to
a simple life-style.

Teach me the contentment that wisely weds
the earthly to the eternal,
now and at the hour of my death.

Retreat Session Two

The Simple Life

On the day after my election, I asked Count dalla Torre, the editor of the Vatican newspaper, *Osservatore Romano,* to come and see me. Someone said he had not had a private meeting with a pope for the last twelve years. I told him I was very interested in the newspaper and its value for the Church, and I promised him I would support him in whatever way I could.

I wanted, however, a small change in the paper's policy of using elaborate adjectives whenever the pope is quoted. I asked the Count to stop using formulas such as "august lips," "illumined by grace," and so on. I asked him just to write, "The pope said so and so, the pope did so and so." Direct and unadorned reporting would be more effective. Alas, I must tell you, the poor count just couldn't do it. He loved those old-fashioned imperial expressions. This would not be the first time my wishes were ignored. As I became fond of saying, "I'm only the pope around here."

My long experience taught me not to get upset over this. I lived by a practical proverb that describes my leadership style: "See everything, correct a little and forget the rest."

I hope you appreciate that I tell these little stories about my life, not out of vanity or self-regard, but to share with you my learning experiences. I like to hear how others learned from life and trust that you do so as well. As you well know, "Good judgment is the product of experience, and experience is the result of bad judgments."

In this retreat we are exploring the theme of wisdom. Scripture teaches that wisdom comes from God who places it in our hearts. "For the Lord gives wisdom; from his mouth come knowledge and understanding;...for wisdom will come into your heart and knowledge will be pleasant to your soul."[1] In other words, wisdom is truth that, by God's grace, moves from the mind to the heart in order to move us to live and act on it.

Such a journey is harder than it sounds. Many say the longest trip is from the head to the heart. The greatest pitfall for intellectuals is to stop at the neck and stay put in the life of the mind. But unless truth is married to love, there will be no wisdom. Notice how often Scripture connects truth and love: "But speaking the truth in love, we must grow up in every way into him who is the head, into Christ."[2] "The elder to the elect lady and her children, whom I love in the truth."[3] "The elder to the beloved Gaius, whom I love in truth."[4]

Today I want to help you see the link between wisdom and a simple life-style. I will organize our thoughts around a few points to ponder.

1. Love the simple life.

> The more mature I grow in years and experience the more I recognize that the surest way to make myself holy and to succeed in the service of the Holy See lies in the constant effort to reduce everything, principles, aims, position, business, to the utmost simplicity and tranquility; I must always take care to strip my vines of all useless foliage and spreading

> tendrils, and concentrate on what is truth, justice and charity, above all charity. Any other way of behaving is nothing but affectation and self-assertion; it soon shows itself in its true colors and becomes a hindrance and a mockery.[5]

When I reached my sixtieth birthday, I said to myself, "I am getting old. I must prepare for death. I should simplify my life." Yet there was always within me a joyful attachment to simplicity. Think of it this way: You have physical and spiritual interests. Material preoccupations are complex. Spiritual ones tend to be simple. Material divides. Spirit unites. You can chop up the physical into many parts like the egg, Humpty Dumpty, which fell from the wall. But you cannot carve up the soul.

Therefore, to enjoy the simplifying force of your soul, you must first calm down the material, bodily and physical side of your life. The consumer society and the information explosion pull you toward the specific, concrete and material, the world of data and the life of self-gratification. This causes the strange illusion, "I am what I own." The material becomes a detour away from the spiritual. I think the title of the book by the English economist, E. F. Schumacher, *Small Is Beautiful*, is a fine motto for our goal. "Less is more" as the modern architects tell us.

> Oh, the simplicity of the Gospel, of *The Imitation of Christ*, of the *Little Flowers* of St. Francis and of the most exquisite passages in St. Gregory, in his *Moralia:* "The simplicity of the just man is derided," and the words that follow! I enjoy these pages more and more and return to them with joy. All the wiseacres of this world, and all the cunning minds, including those in Vatican diplomacy, cut such a poor figure in the light of the simplicity and grace shed by this great and fundamental doctrine of Jesus and his

saints! This is the surest wisdom, that confounds the learning of this world and, with courtesy and true nobility, is consistent, equally well and even better, with the loftiest achievements in the sphere of science, even of secular and social science, in accordance with the requirements of time, place and circumstance. "This is the height of philosophy, to be simple with prudence," as was said by St. John Chrysostom, my great patron saint of the East.[6]

Lord, Jesus, preserve in us the love and practice of simplicity which, by keeping us humble, makes us more like you and draws and saves souls.

2. Follow the four things that bring great peace.

You now know how much I like *The Imitation of Christ.* I call it the "golden book." It was written in the Netherlands between 1420 and 1427 by Thomas á Kempis. It made its way through Europe in Latin, French, German, Italian and Spanish in more than one hundred printed editions by the end of the fifteenth century. In the eighteenth century Samuel Johnson remarked to James Boswell that it "must be a good book, as the world has opened its arms to receive it." Saint Thomas More recommended it as one of the three books every Christian should read. I believe that no book other than the Bible has been so universally read and loved by Christians of all faiths.

One of its most powerful passages pertains to our topic and has been a profound influence on my life. You may find it in Chapter Twenty-three under the title, "Of Four Things that Bring Great Peace." Let me quote it for you. Jesus speaks: "Strive, my friend, to do another's will rather than your own; always prefer to have less than more; always seek the lower place and be submissive in all things; always wish and pray that God's will may be entirely fulfilled in you, for you see, the person who does all this enters a place of peace and rest."[7]

Immense wisdom is packed into this small passage, which contains such shrewd advice for gaining simplicity by imitating Jesus. Ponder with me each of these four invitations.

a) Strive, my friend, to do another's will rather than your own. The world teaches us to get our own way, even at the expense of others. In the creation story Adam and Eve preferred their own will to God's. But in Gethsemane, Jesus submitted to the Father's will. Obedience has become a difficult virtue for modern people. I was taught, "If you want to command, you must first learn how to obey."

Now this advice to do the will of another assumes that the other person is not asking us to do something evil, in which case we would have to refuse to do it. We are talking about everyday matters in which we are training our souls in the discipline of losing our vanity and self-destructive pride. Far from weakening our wills, this has the opposite effect of making them tough and strong.

Saint Paul speaks of the "obedience of faith" (Romans 1:5). The Latin word for obedience means to listen and respond. Faith is listening to what God wants of us; it invites a positive answer. Doing what others want helps us to obey God. I have said we must not do evil. Nor should we avoid what our life's calling evidently is because others want us to do something else. It's all a matter of prudence, isn't it? Prudence and simplicity go together.

b) Always prefer to have less than more. The culture seduces us into thinking we will be happier with more rather than less. According to this philosophy, nothing succeeds like excess. It's not easy to resist this trend, especially when the spirit of society supports it, and all our peers are acquiring more.

Generally, this applies to material goods. But there is also a spiritual gluttony which stuffs the soul and chokes it. When I was in seminary I made a note of this very problem.

> Yesterday my learned professor of Church history gave us excellent advice, particularly useful to me: read little, little but well. And what he said about reading I will apply to everything else: little but well. When I think of all the books I have read in the course of my studies, in the vacations and during my military service! the tomes, periodicals, newspapers! And how much do I remember of all this? Nothing, or almost nothing. All those spiritual works, all those lives of the saints—and what do I remember? Nothing, or almost nothing.
>
> I feel a restless longing to know everything, to study all the great authors, to familiarize myself with the scientific movements in their various manifestations, but in actual fact I read one book, devour another and do not get very far with anything. "Give up trying to know too much, for this is very distracting and may lead you astray."[8]

Always prefer to have less rather than more.

c) Always seek the lower place and be submissive in all things. In my life, I have always sought the last place and have never regretted it. Is this not what Jesus taught us in the parable of the banquet when he counseled us to avoid seeking a seat at the head of the table? Better to look for a humbler place. Then think of how happy you will be when the host says, "Friend, come up higher."

> The sense of my smallness and of my nothingness has always been my good companion, keeping me humble and content and granting me the joy of consecrating myself as best I can to the

uninterrupted exercise of obedience and charity.

I come from humble beginnings, and I was raised in a restraining, blessed poverty whose needs are few and which assures the growth of the highest and noblest virtues, and prepares one for the great ascents of life.[9]

d) Always wish and pray that God's will may be entirely fulfilled in you. Saint Thomas Aquinas teaches that one of the wounds of original sin is weakness in our will. Saint Paul vividly describes his own experience of this condition: "I do not understand my own actions. For I do not do what I want, but I do the very thing I hate."[10] I find it helpful to pray for a strong will each day by saying, "O Jesus, by the mystery of your agony in the garden where you submitted to the Father's will, deliver me from weakness in my will so that I may do the Father's will."

It takes practice and prayer to be able to have God's will achieved in us. My patron, Saint John Chrysostom explains this as well as anyone: "Consider how (Jesus Christ) teaches us to be humble, by making us see that our virtue does not depend on our work alone but on grace from on high. He commands each of the faithful who prays to do so universally, for the whole world."

3. Be a cheerful believer.

Cheerfulness at all times, tranquillity, a mind free from care. When I see that I have kept my resolutions carefully I will praise God from my heart for all he has done; when I have failed I will be careful not to lose heart and I will think that sometimes God permits this to happen so that I may become more humble and entrust myself more wholly to his loving care. After any fault I will make an act of profound humility and then begin again, as cheerfully as ever, smiling as if God had just caressed me, kissed me,

> and raised me up with his own hands—and I will set out once more, confident, joyful, "in the name of the Lord." O good Jesus, you do know how much I desire to love you![11]

Complexity worries us. Simplicity cheers us. I have lived long enough to know there are three great movements in our personal lives. We begin with the simplicity of the child. Then we move to the complexity of adulthood. Finally we return to simplicity in old age, only now our whole life experience is integrated into it. Philosopher Paul Ricoeur imagines the process as a diamond. At the base of the jewel we start our lives with first naivete. In the widest part of the diamond we go through our complex phase. At the summit of the gem we arrive at second naivete.

In the Gospels Jesus urges us to become again like little children, to have their native cheerfulness and their capacity for the wholeness and beauty of God. Allow me to share with you the first vivid memory of my childhood, an experience connected with our Blessed Mother. The Marian shrine in my village was at the end of a rocky road, among the trees where one could not venture further.

It is still a place of pilgrimage today especially for young people going to military service or emigrants setting off for work. The elderly like it, too, because the shrine reminds them of the kindness of Mary who inspires them to hope. My mother brought me there and said, "Look, Angelino, how beautiful Mary is. I have consecrated you wholly to her." This is the first clear memory I have of my childhood. At the age of six I memorized my first poem. I still know it by heart.

> How sweet to the heart
> is your name, Mary.

Every joy I have
comes from your name.
What a fine idea of love
I learned from your name.
What fine desires are kindled
and awakened in my breast.[12]

Have you ever noticed how easily children smile and laugh? They have a spontaneous sense of humor. The cares and responsibilities of life cause too many adults to settle for a humorless attitude. I think God prefers cheerful believers and has given us all we need to use humor to put life's trials in perspective. Yes, I know there is a time to cry, and I have done my share of mourning. But life is not unrelieved sorrow. A saint is a born-again child. I am not attracted to prophets of gloom. Jesus Christ has risen from the dead, conquered evil by his cross and gives us a share in his victory. We have every reason to hope and to be filled with joy at what Jesus is able to accomplish in this world.

At the opening of the Second Vatican Council I spoke against a pessimism that was not worthy of the gift of faith and hope we have received in our baptisms and is nurtured by the continuing presence of the Holy Spirit.

> In the everyday exercise of our pastoral ministry, greatly to our sorrow, we sometimes have to listen to those who although consumed with zeal do not have very much judgment...or balance. To them the modern world is nothing but betrayal and ruination. They claim that this age is far worse than previous ages, and they go on as though they had learned nothing at all from history—and yet history is the great teacher of life.... They behave as though the first five centuries saw a complete vindication of the Christian idea and the Christian cause, and as though religious liberty was never put in jeopardy in

> the past. We feel bound to disagree with these prophets of misfortune...who are for ever forecasting calamity—as though the end of the world were imminent. And yet today Providence is guiding us towards a new order of human relationships which, thanks to human effort and yet far surpassing its hopes, will bring us to the realisation of still higher and undreamed of expectations; in this way even human oppositions can lead to the good of the Church.[13]

Simplicity and humor would have gone a long way to dispel the pessimism of the prophets of gloom. Let us look at the story of Phillip Neri, a cheerful saint, who with deceptive simplicity taught people to smile at human folly.

The Story of God's Clown—Saint Phillip Neri

I am a great lover of history and its lessons. I think of Rome in the tempests caused by the Reformation of the sixteenth century. I recall Saint Phillip Neri who decided not to curse the darkness but to light a candle of hope—and to do it with cheerful humor.

I see him again strolling through Rome wearing his clothes inside out along with floppy white shoes to amuse those who stared at him. He did not mind being God's clown. When Phillip heard that people were impressed with his humble ways, he borrowed a friend's mink coat. Thus robed he paraded through the streets, gesturing like a snob and posturing as though he were full of vanity. The child in Phillip found mischievous ways to achieve his goal, such as occasionally shaving only half his beard, or strutting around with a large, blue cushion on his head.

What a simple and merry man he was! He might arrive at a church wearing an old jacket over his cassock, his biretta cocked on the side of his head, accompanied by a friend instructed to keep brushing nonexistent lint from his clothes. When pompous clergy came to visit him, he entertained them by presenting them with a monkey wearing a clerical hat and carrying a gun.

Once when a delegation of nobility arrived for a visit, Phillip insisted they listen while he read out loud from a joke book written by the Florentine satirist Mainardi. After a few good laughs, he said, "You see how important are the issues which claim my attention." When a disciple of Phillip asked his permission to wear a hair shirt, Phillip agreed—so long as he wore it outside his clothes and not next to his skin. The disciple had not expected this embarrassment which did not suit his self-congratulatory plan. Phillip rightly judged that an itch to one's feelings may well be a greater asceticism than bodily discomfort.

Phillip did not sit around groaning about the threats to the Church, drearily forecasting the end of the world, throwing up his hands in despair at the news reports from the religious battlefields of the day. He lived a simple life-style. When someone tried to plant a cardinal's hat on his head, he gleefully ran away, taking great delight seeing them futilely and breathlessly chasing him. He was a cheerful saint who laughed at ambition and deflated the pompous. He proved that humor and simplicity go together.

Saint Francis of Assisi was the Church's greatest witness to simplicity. He lived poverty of spirit in a way that has enchanted the world ever since. His ability to commune with nature and animals—as well as people—always captivates us.

The *Little Flowers* of Saint Francis never fail to charm me by their simplicity and humor. "I enjoy these pages more and more and return to them with joy."[14] Who better than Saint Francis of Assisi can inspire us to a life of simplicity and faith? Let's listen again to the wonderful story of "The Wolf of Gubbio."

The Story of Saint Francis and the Wolf of Gubbio

When Saint Francis visited Gubbio, the people told him they were upset and terrified by a powerful wolf whose ravenous hunger led him to attack humans as well as animals. Well-armed search parties had tried to trap the wolf and subdue him, but were driven back by his ferocious strength and frightening anger. People were afraid to leave the safety of the town behind its walls.

Francis said that he would go out and meet the wolf. The people warned him that this was too dangerous, "The wolf will attack and kill you." Francis prayed and placed his trust in Jesus, the Lord of the animal world and all creation. Armed only with faith and prayer, Francis searched for the wolf. Some townspeople accompanied him at a distance.

They looked on in horror as they saw the wolf charge at Francis. He blessed the wolf with the sign of the Cross and said, "Come to me, Brother Wolf. In the name of Christ, I order you not to hurt me or anyone else." The wolf stopped his murderous advance on Francis, walked up to him quietly and lay at his feet as though he were a lamb.

Francis spoke to the wolf. "Brother Wolf, you have caused much harm, killing animals and people, terrorizing both the town and the countryside. I want to make peace between you and everyone else. If you agree to join in the peace, I assure you that no one will come after you with swords and dogs to harm you." The wolf showed his willingness to make peace by moving its head and ears and tail.

"I promise you that these people will feed you with all the food you need for the rest of your life. Promise me that you will never again harm any animal or human. Will you promise me that?"

The wolf nodded his head and promised to do what Francis said. "Brother Wolf, give me a pledge that you will do what you say." Francis held out his hand. The wolf raised its paw and put it in Francis' hand. "Brother Wolf, come with me now in the name of Jesus, without fear, into the town and show your face of peace."

The wolf walked beside Francis as though he were a lamb. They came to the town square where the whole population had gathered. Francis preached a sermon about conversion from sin and turning in love toward Jesus Christ. God had permitted the calamity caused by the wolf because of their sinfulness. What the wolf had done would be nothing compared to the fires of hell if they did not reform their lives according to the teachings of Jesus in the Gospels. "Come back to Christ. God will save you from the devouring wolf in this world and hell in the next."

Francis told the people that the wolf had promised peace. He will never hurt you again. "Will you promise to feed him and take care of him?" The people agreed in a loud voice.

Then the wolf arose and put its paw in Francis' hand. The people cheered as the burden of hostility was lifted and a reign of peace was restored.

My dear friends, I need not expand on this lovely message which tells itself so well. No other saint makes us think more of Jesus than Saint Francis. Who else could be a greater example of the simple life which is our message for today? Happily, there are new witnesses today, such as Dorothy Day and Mother Teresa. They prove that God's grace has created contemporary saints of simplicity.

Genius and simplicity go together. Francis was a spiritual genius who clung tenaciously to his simple life-style and taught us how to love each other and all creation with an open mind and an open heart. Commit yourselves to simplicity. Simplify your life. You will never regret it.

For Reflection

1. Love the simple life.

Simplicity is connected with choice. Every choice simplifies your life. Choice means saying no to one path in order to say yes to another. You can't have it all. You must sacrifice. Every choice is a sacrifice of one path for another. Every such choice simplifies your life by at least fifty percent. For every path that is chosen, at least one is rejected, often more than one. The more natural it becomes to you to make moral choices, the more natural it will become to you to live simply.[15]

- *How do you use your time? Do you live by the clock? Or have you learned to live by quality time? There are no clocks in the next world. What can you do to put quality time in your life, the kind of time that is a rehearsal for eternity?*
- *Make a list of what you think are the best things in life. Compare the list to your actual life. What would you let go of to make your life simpler?*

2. Follow the four things that bring you great peace.

Read again this advice from the *Imitation of Christ* found in this chapter on pages 42 to 43.

- *Which of the four things applies to you most at this time in your life? How are you influenced by these principles? What should you do to seek peace through this method?*

3. Be a cheerful believer.

One evening during his tour of duty as nuncio to Paris, Roncalli attended a reception for the heads of the different religious denominations. He met the chief rabbi of Paris. The two discovered they had many common interests and engaged in a long conversation. When dinner was announced they found themselves still talking animatedly to one another at the door of the dining room. Nuncio Roncalli did not like to play the game, "After you; no, after you." He warmly took the arm of the rabbi and steered him into the dining room, first saying, "The Old Testament before the New."

- *The light touch is better than heavy-handedness. How would you rate yourself: too much on the serious side? inclined to a sense of humor? How would you achieve a balance between gravity and light-heartedness?*
- *What are some stories about yourself which show you know how to laugh at your own foolishness?*
- *Why is exaggerated solemnity not a good idea?*
- *Name people who can make you laugh. These can be both people in public life as well as those among your family, friends and acquaintances. How can they help you develop your own sense of humor and a cheerful attitude toward life?*

Closing Prayer

Jesus, you lived the simple life throughout your ministry in Galilee and Judea. You taught simplicity both by example and by your teachings. Move my mind and heart to see the value of the simple life and send your Holy Spirit to guide and strengthen me in the pursuit of this evangelical way of living. Remind me to read the lives of the saints and other outstanding disciples of yours to be inspired by their example. And when I tend to be grim, put a smile in my heart; when I think the going is too tough, make me laugh; when I become overly solemn say to me, "Lighten up." Amen.

Notes

[1] Proverbs 2:6, 10, *NRSV*.

[2] Ephesians 4:15, *NRSV*.

[3] 2 John 1:11, *NRSV*.

[4] 3 John 1:11, *NRSV*.

[5] *Journal of a Soul*, pp. 270-271.

[6] Ibid., p. 271.

[7] Thomas á Kempis, *The Imitation of Christ: A New Reading of the 1441 Latin Autograph Manuscript* by William C. Creasy (Macon, Ga.: Mercer University Press, 1989), p. 81.

[8] *Journal of a Soul*, p. 105.

[9] *Wit and Wisdom of Good Pope John*, collected by Henri Fesquet, trans. Salvator Attanasio (New York: P. J. Kenedy & Sons, 1964), pp. 35-36.

[10] Romans 7:15.

[11] *Journal of a Soul*, p. 96.

[12] *Pope John XXIII*, p. 10.

[13] Ibid., p. 431.

[14] *Journal of a Soul*, p. 271.

[15] Peter Kreeft, *Making Choices: Practical Wisdom for Everyday Moral Decisions* (Ann Arbor, Mich.: Servant Publications, 1990), p. 148.

Day Three

Calm Down

Coming Together in the Spirit

> *"I must always be cheerful, serene, courageous, until my last hour."*

In my early days as pope I had a difficult time eliminating what I considered to be excessive ceremonial. Guido Gusso, one of the veteran reporters from *Osservatore Romano*, insisted on interviewing me while on his knees. I finally had to threaten to leave the room if he refused to sit down. He also followed the old custom of genuflecting three times whenever he came into my study. I wanted him to stop it. "It's a force stronger than I am, Holiness."

"Very well, but once is enough," said I. " Don't you think I believe you the first time?"

When an ambassador from an Arab country arrived to present his credentials, he began by reading a long and predictably flowery speech. I interrupted him at his first pause. "Come, your excellency, let us hand these formal addresses to our aides. Then you and I can go into my library and have a good talk."

Of course, I could not change everything. My chamberlain (chief of protocol), Monsignor Mario Nassali Rocca de Corneliano, had to contend with my egalitarian streak. He looked on in numb amazement as I escorted a visitor from the library through a series of antechambers and all the way out to the stairway leading to the Saint Damasus courtyard.

When I returned, the chamberlain complained that this sort of thing just wasn't done. People came to the pope, and he received them and bade them farewell in his quarters. "But this is my house," I said. "I am merely showing a guest to the door." Nonetheless, I lost the battle. Soon after, I shook a visitor's hand at the door of my library and said, "I'd like to show you out, but Monsignor Nasalli Rocca doesn't like me to do that."

Defining Our Thematic Context

Wise People Live Simply

In this retreat we are trying to find ways to receive the gift of God's wisdom. We have looked at the role of love in this process on Day One. Day Two we pondered simplicity of life as a method for openness to wisdom.

In our meditation points I asked you to consider these principles: (1) Love the simple life. (2) Follow the four things that bring great peace, these being found in the twenty-third chapter of *The Imitation of Christ*. (3) Be a cheerful believer.

Let us pray for the Holy Spirit's help as we continue our retreat.

Opening Prayer

Holy Spirit, on Easter night
Jesus breathed you upon the apostles
and filled them with your divine calm.
Breathe on us, breath of God,
to reconcile us with you, others and ourselves,

that we may have the inner peace for which we long.
Holy Spirit, at Pentecost you came in wind and fire
to take away our fear and bring us your love.
Reveal to us how to find inner calm
and rest in your presence.
Breathe on us, breath of God,
so that our bodies and souls
will glow with your fire divine.

Retreat Session Three

Perplexity and Pain

In my thirty-ninth year I received an invitation to become the national director of the Italian office for the Propagation of the Faith. The letter came from Cardinal Van Rossum, head of the Propaganda; today this is the office for the Evangelization of Peoples. This organization is designed to create interest in and raise money for the Church's foreign missions. They were looking for an organizer, a fund-raiser and someone who would arouse enthusiasm for the missions.

The invitation caused me "perplexity and pain," as I wrote in my journal. I was happy in Bergamo. I wasn't sure I'd be happy in Rome. At the same time I did not want to resist the will of God, if that really was God's will. Of course, I was devoted to the Church's mission efforts, but I felt a mistake had been made. I did not consider myself a good organizer, nor did I believe I had the right temperament for the post. I'm someone who doesn't get much done. By nature I'm lazy. I write slowly, and I'm easily distracted in my work.

> The active life of exterior movement to which I have so far been condemned was never my ideal; I would have preferred a life of recollection and study in a monastic cell, with a taste for the direct ministry of souls but peacefully and without fuss.[1]

I asked my bishop what he thought. He approved the idea but said replacing me would not be easy. He wanted a delay in the appointment. I also wrote to my good friend, Cardinal Ferrari, archbishop of Milan, and asked him to advise me on this decision. In his written reply he urged me to take the job.

> You know how much I love you: it is another debt towards Mgr. Radini Tedeschi. Precisely for that reason, here is my clear and unhesitating judgement: the will of God is as plain as can be, since the "red" pope (the Prefect of Propaganda) is the echo of the "white" pope; and both are of God. So go ahead. Whenever God calls, one goes, without hesitation, abandoning oneself in everything to his divine and living Providence.[2]

Ferrari's letter dissolved my doubts, and I accepted the appointment. I share this story with you as a small example of how God led me through a troubled decision and brought peace to my heart.

As you can see, I trusted in the wisdom of people I respected in making my decision. Listen to one of my favorite Scripture passages:

> Stand in the company of the elders.
> Who is wise? Attach yourself to such a one.
> Be ready to listen to every godly discourse,
> and let no wise proverbs escape you....
> Do not ignore the discourse of the aged,
> for they themselves learned from their parents;
> from them you learn how to understand

and to give an answer when the need arises.[3]

As we try to unravel the beauty of wisdom and the joy it promises for our lives, I suggest we turn our attention to the role of inner peace. Wise people certainly experience turmoil, but they have learned to achieve serenity in the storm. Here are some ways in which this can happen.

1. Cultivate patience.

I was the first papal representative to Bulgaria in six hundred years because the country was under the rule of the Ottoman Empire during that time. Most Bulgarians belonged to the Orthodox Church. The majority of Catholics were Eastern rite, while several thousand were Latin rite. After twenty months of visiting all the parishes in the country, I went to Rome to make a report.

I pointed out that in Bulgaria, ecclesiastical responsibility was divided among foreign religious orders—the Capuchins, Assumptionists and Passionists. Schools and hospitals were run by nuns of those orders from France, Italy and Switzerland. Because of this, Bulgarian Catholics viewed their Church as a mission church subordinate to other countries. I judged that we needed to develop local leadership and a native clergy.

I proposed that a Bulgarian priest, Father Stefan Kurteff, whom I had come to know and admire, be made a bishop of the Eastern rite Catholics and that a seminary be built to train priests for both the Eastern and Latin rites. I had many other suggestions, all designed to bring the Catholic Church in Bulgaria closer to those most concerned with it. I returned to Sofia, the capital, and waited in vain. Except for making Father Kurteff a bishop, all my other ideas were ignored.

I wrote to Rome asking what happened, but received no reply. I received no further instructions about what my pastoral duties would be now that Kurteff was basically in charge of most of the Catholics. Frankly, I had nothing to do, and I was being ignored. I tried to bear this patiently but was inwardly distressed. I wrote to a friend in the Vatican about my problems, and the letter came to the attention of certain Church officials who were displeased about what I said.

So I wrote again, this time asking forgiveness in case I offended anyone, then proceeded to write twenty typewritten pages on the subject of difficulties caused me by my Roman superiors. Somehow this letter arrived on the desk of Pope Pius XI. "Behold the wrath of the lamb!" he said. But nothing was done.

To my diary I confided:

> I have been a Bishop for twenty months. As I clearly foresaw, my ministry has brought me many trials. But, and this is strange, these are not caused by the Bulgarians for whom I work but by the central organs of ecclesiastical administration. This is a form of mortification and humiliation that I did not expect and which hurts me deeply....
>
> I must, I will accustom myself to bearing this cross with more patience, calm and inner peace than I have so far shown. I shall be particularly careful in what I say to anyone about this. Every time I speak my mind about it I take away from the merit of my patience. "Set a guard over my mouth, O Lord." I shall make this silence, which must be, according to the teaching of St. Francis de Sales, meek and without bitterness, an object of my self-examinations.[4]

I learned patience and obtained inner peace by intensifying my prayer, reducing worry and putting greater control on my speech. I gave greater attention to my religious duties: Holy Mass, the Breviary, reading the

Scriptures, meditation, examination of conscience, the daily rosary, visits to the Blessed Sacrament.

The value of religious exercises cannot be underestimated. Just as physical exercise tones the body, strengthens the heart and increases circulation, so spiritual exercises on a daily basis, faithfully adhered to, tone the soul, strengthen mind and will, and increase our capacity for virtue. The extent of these exercises in our lives must depend on how deeply we are responding to God's call and the circumstances in which we find ourselves. But there is no doubt that daily prayer, generally at set times, is essential for inner peace and patience.

Listen to Saint John Vianney's wonderful words on prayer:

> My little children, your hearts are small, but prayer stretches them and makes them capable of loving God.... How often we come to church with no idea of what to do or what to ask for. And yet, whenever we go to any human being, we know well enough why we go. And still worse, there are some who seem to speak to the good God like this: "I will only say a couple of things to you, and then I will be rid of you." I often think that when we come to adore the Lord, we would receive everything we ask for, if we would ask with a living faith and with a pure heart.[5]

Secondly, you will experience more tranquility and patience by not worrying so much about whether you are doing all the good you think is necessary for the benefit of others. So long as you are acting responsibly toward others, always with the motive of love, that is sufficient. God knows how to use everything for the advancement of the Kingdom, even your inability to do more or the frustrations you experience due to the opposition of others.

Jesus asks us to give up needless anxiety. "Therefore, I

tell you, do not worry about your life, what you will eat or what you will drink, or about your body, what you will wear.... Look at the birds of the air; they neither sow nor reap nor gather into barns, and yet your heavenly Father feeds them. Are you not of more value than they?"[6]

Thirdly, control of the tongue will bring you more peace than you can imagine. That has been hard for me since I am an incorrigibly talkative person. It is my nature to talk too much. This is a gift from God but should be handled with moderation and respect. I know how important the mastery of the tongue is.

> I will be more and more careful to rule my tongue. I must be more guarded in the expression of my opinions, even with persons of my own household. This must once more become the object of the particular examinations of conscience. Nothing must escape my lips other than praise or the most mildly expressed disapproval or general exhortations to charity, to the apostolate, to virtuous living.[7]

Finally, I recommend a regular examination of conscience as a way of learning patience. It has been said that the unexamined life is not worth living. I assume the author meant that the fullness of living is missed if it is never reflected upon. We are the only creatures on earth who can think about ourselves. This is one of our greatest gifts.

Choose a time each day to review your life, what bothers you, how you have treated others, how they have reacted to you, what brought you joy, where you need improvement. Talk over your life with God, asking for the graces needed to be patient, loving, peaceful. Make resolutions to improve despite countless setbacks. Ask the Lord for serenity through a life of self-giving and self-sacrifice. Bring peace and tranquility to others. The more you do this, the more calm you will feel.

2. Learn the obedience of faith.

Saint Paul writes that the proclamation of Jesus Christ is made known to the Gentiles "according to the command of the eternal God, to bring about the obedience of faith" (Romans 16:26). I quote this for you because there is a vital connection between faith, obedience and inner peace. It just so happens that my bishop's motto is *Obedientia et Pax* ("Obedience and Peace")—an expression I borrowed from a daily saying of my favorite Church historian, Caesare Baronius. One of my most painful Bulgarian experiences may drive this point home.

At the beginning of 1930, five years into my tour of duty in Bulgaria, King Boris announced he was marrying Princess Giovanna, daughter of King Victor Emmanuel of Italy. Before the Church could dispense her to enter a mixed marriage with an Orthodox king, guarantees were needed that there would be a wedding ceremony according to the laws of the Church and that any children born would be raised Catholics. I was entrusted with the delicate mission of winning King Boris's agreement.

I appreciated his problem. Eighty-five percent of his people were Orthodox, and they would wonder why their king had to submit to Catholic conditions—and the Orthodox hierarchy would question the sincerity of his faith if he were not married in their Church. Worse yet the newspapers speculated about this every day and heated arguments were heard on street corners.

After many weeks of persistent and gentle persuasion, I finally obtained the king's agreement, and he signed the papers. I still worried something would go wrong. It did. The royal wedding was held on October 25 in Assisi according to the Catholic rite. Six days later, as soon as the couple had returned to Sofia, Boris insisted that he and Giovanna submit to an Orthodox ceremony in their cathedral of St. Alexander Nevsky. He said it was only a "nuptial blessing," though the sacrament was repeated.

I felt betrayed. I called on Signor Piacenti, the Italian ambassador to Bulgaria, and registered a strong protest. Piacenti said to me, "Don't take it too seriously, Your Excellency. Actually, King Boris professes the Orthodox faith, and the matter is one for his conscience. As to Queen Giovanna, who is a Catholic, well, it means she will go to confession." I need not tell you how angry I was. Piacenti simply rang a bell and told the footman to accompany the "Vatican representative" to his car.

Things got worse. I was summoned to Rome and brought immediately to the papal apartments. Pope Pius did not allow me to speak. I was kept on my knees while he angrily rebuked me. He said it was my fault that the Church was compromised in the eyes of the world. The Holy See had counted on me and I had failed. I should have seen through Boris's conspiracy and even the complicity of Giovanna. I should have warned against granting the dispensation. He implied I was too naive about the whole affair.

I was suffering and heartsore on many accounts. Boris had deceived me. I was convinced that Giovanna was an innocent victim of the affair. And I was not allowed to explain myself to the pope.

This story has a few more twists and turns. The happily married Boris, more confident about his standing with the Orthodox Church, felt conciliatory toward the Vatican and allowed its representative a higher diplomatic standing. I was elevated from Apostolic Visitor to Apostolic Delegate. This also meant I could finally move to a larger and more decent house. Then, on January 13, 1933, Queen Giovanna gave birth to a daughter. The following day, the king, violating another promise he had made, had the baby baptized in the royal chapel with an Orthodox ceremony. I had warned Rome earlier that this would probably happen.

I believed that the queen was not responsible and confirmed this in an interview with her. She said the king came to her apartment that day after the birth and took the baby for the baptism. Her mother was en route from Italy to become godmother at what she thought would be a Catholic baptism. I advised Giovanna to attend Mass for the time being at the Delegation Chapel lest she be harassed by antagonistic Catholics at St. Joseph's.

As the closing note of this story, I was again called to a private audience with the pope. By this time he understood that I had done what is right and proper all along. "Now we should get up and excuse ourselves with you," the pope said gently, "but if God should ever will you should sit upon this chair, you will know that is not possible." Then he rose. "As pope, no, but as Achille Ratti, yes. As Achille Ratti, I stand, and I ask you to pardon me. I give you my hand in friendship."

I believe this extended narrative will help you see how I tried to live out my motto, "Obedience and Peace." It was clearly not easy. I hope to die with the satisfaction of having always, even in the smallest things, honored my obligation to find peace through obedience. I tell you all this so you may find light in Saint Paul's beautiful expression, "the obedience of faith." If I did not have faith I could not have adhered to the will of God as manifested to me by the Church during my long Way of the Cross in Bulgaria.

> One of the similes used by St. Francis de Sales, which I love to repeat, is: "I am like a bird singing in a thicket of thorns"; this must be a continual inspiration to me. So, I must say very little to anyone about the things that hurt me. Great discretion and forbearance in my judgments of men and situations: willingness to pray particularly for those who may

> cause me suffering, and in everything great kindness and endless patience.... So long as charity may triumph, at all costs, I would choose to be considered as of little worth. I will be patient and good to a heroic degree, even if I am to be crushed. Only in this way shall I deserve to be called a true Bishop and be worthy to share in the priesthood of Jesus Christ, who at the cost of his compliance, humiliation and suffering was the real and only physician and Saviour of all mankind, by whose wounds we are healed.[8]

I urge you to consider the importance of faith and obedience as you seek to acquire inner peace and calm. You surely have lived long enough now to know that life is a series of tests, trials that come in your families, marriages, from your children and from your friends and professional colleagues—not to mention breakdowns in health, economic difficulties and other sorrows. These are the forms of the Cross presented to you. These are ways in which Jesus says to you: Lose yourself. Take the Cross. Follow me. This is Christ's invitation to discipleship and it is always connected to the third petition of the Our Father, "Thy will be done."

The will of God will always include the Cross for us just as it did for Jesus whom we follow. Hidden within the glorious Cross is the seed of immense joy, peace, calm and resurrection. "For we walk by faith, not by sight."[9]

Only a living, conscious and active faith in Jesus Christ, his person and his message can reveal the role of obedience to God's will to you. Faith is a response to God revealing his person and message to you. When we truly hear God, we say, "I believe in you. I love you. I will do what you ask of me." This is the interpersonal aspect of faith. All the same you never believe alone because your faith is within the context of the Church's community in which you say with all believers, "We believe in God." Hence your faith is strengthened by the voices, witness and fervor of all members of the community of believers. Such faith is a dialogue of love.

Our faith is always a gift of the Holy Spirit who prompts us to believe and introduces us to the wonder of God's love. As faith develops in our lives, we should experience a growing assurance and conviction about our relationship to God. Read again Chapter Eleven of Hebrews which is a magnificent hymn about faith and the heroes and heroines of the Bible who practiced it so well. Listen to the encouraging and hope-filled first verse and repeat it often to yourself. "Now faith is the assurance of things to be hoped for, the conviction of things not seen."[10]

Our faith is a free response to God who does not impose himself upon us, but proposes to us as a loving spouse asking us for a union of love. And finally, our faith is belief in a message, given in revelation and taught to us authoritatively by the magisterium (the teaching office) of the Church. This message is a word of truth, but recall that the Hebrew word for truth is *emeth,* meaning that truth is more than an abstract principle; it must be practiced and lived in order to be truly accepted and understood. Saint Anselm teaches us that we should have a faith that constantly seeks understanding. "I believe in order that I may understand." But our intellectual understanding of the truths of faith will be greater the more we try to live what we believe, love God, neighbor and self more intensely, and be ready to carry the Cross that leads to the resurrection for which we hope so profoundly.

I have offered you this brief exhortation about faith because it is essential to understanding Paul's inspiring words about the "obedience of faith." May I add here that the word obedience comes from the Latin *obaudire,* meaning to hear and follow. In this process, which I have been unfolding for you, the hearing is a faith-listening to God in order to discern God's will. As you can conclude from my experience, I have seen in the guidance of the Church a way of discovering what is God's will, and that has been immensely fruitful for me.

3. Don't be fearful.

In your search for inner peace you must let go of your fear. Scared and nervous people are not going to be calm. Read how often the angels who are sent by God to earth say, "Be not afraid." When Mary was perplexed by the angel's visit at the Annunciation, she heard Gabriel say, "Do not be afraid, Mary" (Luke 1:30).

The best reason for abandoning fear is that fear prevents you from loving and being loved. Saint John teaches this clearly. "There is no fear in love, but perfect love casts out fear; for fear has to do with punishment, and whoever fears has not reached perfection in love" (1 John 4:18).

I have found that one of the simplest ways of rooting out fear in my life is to put other people at ease. I recall meeting with Rabbi Herbert Friedman and a representation of 130 American Jews. Since they looked a bit intimidated, I wanted to put them at ease, so I greeted them by saying, "I am your brother Joseph." I went on to say, "I am your brother. Certainly there is a difference between those who admit only the Old Testament as their guide and those who add the New Testament as the supreme law and guide. But that distinction does not abolish the brotherhood that comes from a common origin.... We come from the Father, and must return to the Father."[11]

I had many opportunities to take the fear out of people when they came to meet me. When American Congressman Brooks Hays arrived and nervously blurted,

"I'm a Baptist,"[12] I smiled and replied, "Well, I'm John."[13] To the president of Turkey, I spoke a greeting in his language, remembering my years in Istanbul, and concluded, "May God guard you and roses bloom along your way."[14] And when a large group came from the working-class district of Rome, I assured them: "You have not come to see the son of a king, or an emperor, or one of the greats of this earth, but only a priest, the son of poor people, who was called by the Lord and carries the burden of being the supreme pontiff."[15]

If you feel the need to frighten and intimidate other people, I suggest that may be a sign that you are fearful yourself. Fear begets fear just as love engenders love. Would it not be better to let go of your fear and learn how to make others feel at home in your presence? Fear disturbs your inner calm and destroys tranquility.

Now you may rightly tell me that Scripture says, "The fear of the Lord is the beginning of wisdom" (Psalm 111:10). That is true, but the Scripture is speaking of what I would call "good fear," a fear of sinning, of being separated from the love of Christ, of engaging in self-destructive behavior. This is wise fear, related to prudent and sensible caution.

But I am speaking of "bad fear," the kind that is foolish and unnecessary, the type that erodes our relationships with God, others and self, fearfulness when there is no need for it. I am thinking of the four fears that people should try to overcome: fear of failure, rejection, pain and death. I fully acknowledge we all have such fears, but I argue these should be conquered. People who fear failure will never accomplish much because success usually comes only after many mistakes and frustrating attempts.

Those who fear rejection will be rejected. The best way to face this problem is to concentrate on accepting others and making them feel welcome. Those who pay too much attention to their fear of pain will never relax and only suffer all the more.

Those who are so afraid of death that they resolve never to think of it will be mightily surprised when death arrives at the door and, unhappily, they will find themselves unprepared for this event of paramount importance. Since I turned sixty, I have resolutely thought of my forthcoming death and have thought of many ways to prepare properly for it. I do not find this a morbid preoccupation, quite the opposite; it brings me the kind of excitement I have had so many times when embarking on a new journey to see new places. I am preparing for heaven.

So, dear friends, let go of your self-defeating fears, and let love fill the vacuum left by those worrisome anxieties. You will be amazed at how much inner peace fills your hearts when fear is no longer making you miserable. Calm down and your heart will be lifted up, and you will be a joy to your family, friends and all who have the good fortune to know you.

For Reflection

1. Cultivate patience.

"Let everyone be quick to listen, slow to speak, slow to anger" (James 1:19). There are many paths to patience and one of the most effective is control of the tongue. Angry, cynical and thoughtless words disturb the listeners and trouble the speaker. We must learn to rule our tongues if we expect to have serenity. "The tongue is a small member, yet it boasts of great exploits. How great a forest is set ablaze by a small fire. And the tongue is a fire" (James 3:5-6).

- *Read all of James 3, which is his meditation on the need to tame the tongue. A disciplined speech will teach you patience and calm you down.*
- *Each evening reflect on the day's conversations. What words do you wish you hadn't said? How many times did you fail to listen but were quick to speak? What have you learned from this experience?*

2. Learn the obedience of faith.

Pope John XXIII suffered several times at the hands of Church authorities as was illustrated by the stories from his Bulgarian assignment. For most of the ten years he spent there, he felt misunderstood and abandoned by his superiors. Yet throughout it all, he grew in the virtue of patience, obediently did what he was asked and was given the gift of deeper faith. For him it was an extended lesson in discerning and complying with the will of God.

- *What can you learn from him to help you discover God's will in your life? Who are the people, if any, who misunderstand you and treat you unfairly? How can these occasions help you learn the obedience of faith?*
- *How confident are you that you act toward others in a fair and sympathetic manner? If you need improvement here, what should you do?*
- *Why is a living, conscious and active faith in Jesus Christ essential for the obedience of faith?*

3. Don't be fearful.

Some people take too much pleasure in bullying others. Perhaps they have too much fear in their lives. Those who go around intimidating others are troublemakers and simply mire themselves more in fear. They sink further into the storms of their own inner lives.

One of the great messages of Scripture is, "Be not afraid." Why? Because love is letting go of fear.

- *Do you enjoy putting other people at ease, or do you like to make them afraid of you? If you are bent on putting fear in others, how do you do it? Why do you do it? What could you do to stop it?*
- *What do you notice about the "fear factor" in people who are loving and affectionate?*
- *Offer this prayer daily: "The Lord is my light and my salvation, of whom should I be afraid?"*

Closing Prayer

Loving Jesus, you calmed the waves in the storm at sea; please quiet the turbulence within my soul. You exhibited great patience in teaching and training your apostles; show me how to acquire patience especially by ruling my tongue. You perfectly demonstrated what the obedience of faith should be like, especially at Gethsemane when you said, "Not my will but yours be done"; grant me the gift of surrender to God's will. You treated all people with dignity and love; show me how to love everyone and put them at ease. Amen.

Notes

[1] *Pope John XXIII*, p. 101.

[2] Ibid.

[3] Sirach 6:34-35; 8:9, *NRSV*.

[4] *Journal of a Soul*, p. 208.

[5] *The Liturgy of the Hours* (New York: Catholic Book Publishing Co.,

1975), vol. 3, pp. 1573-1574.

[6] Matthew 6:25-26, *NRSV*.

[7] *Journal of a Soul*, p. 210.

[8] Ibid., p. 218.

[9] Corinthians 5:7, *NRSV*.

[10] Hebrews 11:1, *NRSV*.

[11] *Journal of a Soul*, p. 193.

[12] Lawrence Elliott, *I Will Be Called John: A Biography of Pope John XXIII* (New York: Reader's Digest Press, E. P. Dutton & Co., Inc., 1973), pp. 274-275.

[13] Ibid.

[14] Ibid.

[15] Ibid.

DAY FOUR

Walk a Humble Path

Coming Together in the Spirit

> *"For myself, I must think only of remaining very humble, leaving everything else to God."*

After my election as pope, it was clear to me that I must avoid the cult of personality. I tried to remember that underneath the crown and splendid robes lives Angelo Roncalli, whose people worked the land of Lombardy for many generations. Once when visiting a hospital, I was surrounded by a group of nursing sisters who presented me with a white skullcap. It was customary to give them mine in exhange. I refused as gently as I could.

> I will not give you my cap for two reasons.... The first is that I have no wish to create need for a capmaker with nothing more to do than make caps for the pope. And the second is that this sort of thing can lead you into idolatry and superstition.[1]

I loved to walk in the Vatican gardens. This caused a problem for the caretakers of St. Peter's. My predecessor also liked to stroll in the garden, but he always did it at the same hour every day, during which time the caretakers would close the cupola of the basilica to the public. This is an outdoor balcony near the top of St. Peter's dome and from it people could see into the Vatican gardens. My habits were unpredictable, and they did not know what to do.

"Why must you do anything?" I asked. "Why must you close the cupola at all?"

"Because otherwise they would see you, Holiness! The people, all the tourists," replied one of the workers.

I paused for a moment and then said, "Don't worry about it. I promise not to do anything that would scandalize them."[2]

Custom required that the pope wear red velvet slippers everywhere. I could hardly expect to take good walks in these, so I hired a shoemaker to make me sturdy leather walking shoes—and dye them red! Soon I heard people were calling me, "Johnny Walker."

Defining Our Thematic Context

Wise People Seek Serenity

As we travel the path of wisdom in this retreat, we have seen the importance of love and simplicity. We also examined the value of serenity and its relationship to wisdom on Day Three. I asked you to consider these three ways to achieve inner peace: (1) Cultivate patience. (2) Learn the obedience of faith. (3) Don't be scared. Today we will see the connection between humility and wisdom. First, let us ask divine guidance for this meditation.

Opening Prayer

Jesus, you have said to us,
"Learn from me, for I am gentle
and humble of heart" (Matthew 11:29).
Teach us, Lord, how to imitate your humility.

Take away our pride and give us the gift of your humility.
Help us to avoid acting from selfish ambition or conceit.
Unfold for us the mystery of your self-emptying
wherein you left the sanctuary of divinity and
came to live among us.
You humbled yourself and became obedient unto death,
even death on a cross.
Lead us through this mystery so that we too will
walk a humble path.

RETREAT SESSION FOUR

Two Critical Decisions

The morning after my election I had two critical decisions to make: the choice of a secretary of state and the selection of my confessor. I asked Monsignor Domenico Tardini to meet me right after breakfast. He and Monsignor Montini (later Pope Paul VI) had been "sub-secretaries" of state for Pius XII, who acted as his own secretary of state. He was my immediate superior during my assignments to Turkey and Paris.

Tardini had never been one of my admirers and often disapproved of me. Of me he once wrote about my diplomatic judgment, "This fellow has understood nothing." He did not support my appointment as nuncio to Paris. When I met with him after my Paris assignment to thank him for it, he would not accept my thanks nor compliment me. He said he had no part in the appointment which was the direct decision of the pope—which I later found out to be true from Pius XII himself. So this is the man I wanted for my secretary of state. I said to him:

> Now the roles are reversed; tonight I can ask obedience of you.... You've had forty years of service in the immediate entourage of the pope; you've been a faithful servant and priest; you know the problems; you had the confidence of my predecessor; I can't imagine you pensioned off and in retirement. I'll be loyal to you, and you'll be loyal to me. The Lord will guide us.[3]

Tardini raised a number of objections. He said, "New policies need new people. I have frequently disagreed with you in the past. I am tired and my health is getting worse. I want to give myself entirely to my orphan boys at Villa Nazareth." I listened and let him know I understood, but I said, "I want you to take the post." He finally agreed and offered me his obedience.

Next, I discussed with him another vital appointment. I wanted a good confessor and spiritual director. He gave me some names to think about. I prayed and reflected about this and chose, unhesitatingly, Monsignor Alfredo Cavagna. He was two years older than I, a good and holy priest, knew the Roman scene well and could counsel me on other matters. I have made my confession to him ever since on Friday afternoons at 3 o'clock, the day and hour of Jesus' death. I view my weekly confession with great seriousness. It is an excellent way of reviewing my life, week by week, in the light of the demands of the Holy Spirit.

I should think it is clear to you, dear friends, that I needed to swallow my pride and think of the good of the Church in my selection of Tardini. I could have picked from several of my more congenial friends, but my first goal was to serve the Church. I needed an experienced professional, someone who would help me understand the workings of the Curia (the general administration of the Vatican). It was a good choice.

I praise God who has done much to teach and enable me to walk the humble path. On my own this would not have been possible. How often I have prayed, "Jesus, meek and humble of heart, make my heart like unto thine." I know there is an essential link between humility and wisdom. When you think about it, the immense attractiveness of wise people is their humility and not just their shrewdness of judgment. Humility is one of the stars in the crown of wisdom. I urge you to join me in dining at the feast of wisdom.

> Wisdom has built her house...she has also set her table...
> To those without sense she says,
> "Come, eat of my bread and drink of the wine I have mixed.
> Lay aside immaturity and walk in the way of insight."[4]

Humility leads to genuine maturity and insight. The following steps may help you make this journey.

1. Consider pride a blind guide.

The pride of which I speak here is not the legitimate pride parents take in their children, or citizens take in their flag, or athletes in their hard-won victory, or soldiers in their courage, or an actress in a fine performance, or a businesswoman in her leadership ability. Good pride is an honest and modest recognition of excellence and quality.

The pride which is a blind guide is sinful pride, the first of the capital sins. It is the very opposite of humility because it is boastful, vain, imperious, swaggering, and if the truth be said, ridiculous. Proud people are neither humble nor wise. Nor are they particularly likeable. One reason why such proud people lack insight is that they are too self-absorbed; they fail to notice what others really think, nor do they care. They do not know how to listen to the thoughts and judgments of others and basically do not believe anyone has anything to tell them. And even if they seek counsel, it is only for the purpose of advancing their own agendas, which they will aggressively promote no matter what anyone thinks.

One of the best antidotes for a proud person is to find a wise guide. In the days of my youth at the Roman seminary, I was blessed by the arrival of an extraordinary spiritual father, Reverend Francesco Pitocchi, a Redemptorist priest. As a young man he had hoped to become a Jesuit, but the Order asked him to wait. He went on to be ordained a diocesan priest and joined the Redemptorists ten years later. He edited the correspondence of Saint Alphonsus Ligouri, founder of the Order, and published the saint's maxims under the title, "Certain Paradise."

At the age of 43 his health broke down. Digestive troubles and spasms in his neck made him a permanent invalid. He was unable to have any regular parish ministry. However, he did offer occasional retreat and spiritual guidance. He became my spiritual director for twenty-six years until his death. Unintentionally, he provided me with one of my more humbling experiences. I had just been ordained, and he asked me to give a sermon on the Immaculate Conception to the Children of Mary in a rich Roman suburb. I worked hard on the talk, but it did not turn out well.

My talk was a disaster. I mixed up quotations from

> the Old and the New Testaments. I confused St. Alphonsus with St. Bernard. I mistook writings of the Fathers for writings of the prophets. A fiasco. I was so ashamed that afterwards I fell into the arms of Fr. Francesco [Pitocchi] and confessed my mortification.[5]

I used to see Father Pitocchi when he came to the seminary, generally twice a week. He listened to me with great kindness but did not say very much. Often he contented himself with giving me a thought from Scripture. I believe this man of God really cared for each of the seminarians. He paid attention to our weaknesses and our small efforts to overcome them, which he supported with fatherly affection. I wrote a tribute in loving memory of Father Pitocchi soon after his death. You can see from these lines how much he meant to me.

> At the conclusion of our first meeting he gave me a motto to repeat to myself calmly and frequently: *God is all: I am nothing,* and this was like a new principle that opened to my gaze new horizons, unexplored, full of mystery and spiritual beauty....
>
> From that evening onwards I began to understand more clearly than ever before that the life of the spirit is more than just a succession of acts, the natural result of a good character and of a very Christian education strengthened by the Lord's grace; it is rather the gradual formation of habits of thought and action, in the light of higher principles which are revealed to the soul gradually; it is a life that has to be studied and practised like an exact science, the science of the saints, indispensable for anyone who, as he grows older and prepares himself for the priestly ministry, wishes to do honour to his own vocation of saving and sanctifying the souls of his brothers.[6]

Pitocchi showed me that the spiritual life is a slow process of growth in which effective habits of thought and behavior are acquired in the light of principles that become clearer as life goes on. A wise guide is a superb antidote to the blindness of pride.

2. Be down to earth.

Someone once told me that she knew a person who was so heavenly minded that he was no earthly good. It was a shrewd observation. Spirituality does demand heavenly thinking because we must act in accordance with the divine will, but it never forgets the human dimension nor the fact that the will of God is fulfilled here on earth. The very meaning of the Incarnation is that the Son of God came down to earth. Our goal is heaven, but the journey there happens here. Humility is a word that derives from the Latin *humus,* meaning earth. Humble people are "down to earth" people.

The saints of the Church display this earthiness that is characteristic of humility. The celebrated anecdote about Saint Teresa of Avila is a case in point. Tired and agitated during a long coach ride, she was thrown into the mud when the coach overturned. Exasperated, she said to God, "Why do you treat me this way?" "I always deal with my friends in this manner." "Then it's no surprise you have so few!"

Teresa showed she was an earthy mystic in many other ways. While working on the details of a new Carmel at Medina, Teresa was approached by the prior of the male Carmelite monastery who was interested in reforming his own lax friars. The prior was accompanied by a short, frail, young Carmelite. Teresa remarked afterwards, "Bless the Lord, for I have a friar and a half for my new monastery." The little man was John Alvarez, destined to be the famed John of the Cross, the crown and glory of the

Discalced Carmelite friars.

This mystical Teresa spent a lot of time on earthly matters. She argued with zoning boards, settled wills, negotiated purchases and offered down-home advice, as in the case of the Cistercian nun who was collapsing into lengthy trances for no apparent reason. Teresa looked into the matter, as one given to extensive trances herself, and found out the woman was suffering from malnutrition due to ill-advised fasting. "Feed the lady and she'll get better." And she did, never again to have a trance.

One of Teresa's most challenging assignments involved assuming the leadership of the Convent of the Incarnation where she had spent twenty years as a sister before launching her new reformed order. She was being forced on them against their will, and they did not like it. One account reports that the 130 nuns arose in their choir stalls, shouting, weeping and protesting the violation of their voting rights. The provincial remained firm and insisted that Teresa would be prioress.

When the sisters assembled the next morning to hear Teresa's opening remarks, they looked in disbelief at the chair of the prioress upon which stood a statue of the Virgin Mary, with the keys of the convent in her folded hands. Teresa sat on an adjoining chair and delivered an address that was a masterpiece of tact and Christian affection.

> My sisters, this election has distressed me, for it has deprived you of your freedom of choice and given you a prioress against your will, a prioress who would be accomplishing a great deal if she could succeed in learning from each of you here all the good that is in you.
>
> I come solely to serve you and please you in every possible way that I can. See then, my friends, what I can do for each of you,...for though I have lived

> among and governed nuns who are Discalced [Sisters] (of the Strict Observance), I know well enough the way to govern those who are not. I hope the Lord will greatly assist me to do this.[7]

Over the next three years of her tenure, Teresa won their confidence, respect and love as she succeeded in restoring the financial and spiritual matters of the convent.

Teresa's maxims further illustrate her down-to-earth approach to life.

> A prioress may be very holy, yet incapable of governing a community. In that case she should simply be removed from office.
> Never be obstinate, especially in unimportant matters.
> Be kind to others but severe on yourself.
> Everything passes; God never changes.
> Patience obtains all.
> Whoever has God, wants for nothing.
> God alone is enough.[8]

Saint Teresa shows us that humility is not a foolish, groveling, timid, slope-shouldered, tentative, furrowed brow or false modesty virtue. It is down to earth in the best sense of the word. She was able to do this because she was in a proper relationship with God in which she could see the difference between God and herself. She experienced the glorious majesty of God, the incredible beauty and splendor of the divine. Odd as it may seem that is the clue which helped her and will help you to be down to earth.

A true perception of the immensity of God allows us to have a realistic perspective about ourselves. In prayer we slowly become aware of the oceanic love of God and contrast that to the thimblefull of love that we find in ourselves.

Yet the experience should not discourage us because God lets us know how precious we are in his eyes, so beloved that the Son of God became one of us, ate and drank with us, healed people and taught the truths of the Kingdom, submitted to the unjust sentence of death and endured the sufferings of the passion and Cross to demonstrate how deeply God loves us.

3. Gain insight into yourself.

Humble people know themselves. They do not overestimate their abilities. They are remarkably honest about their talents and are gifted with a strong sense of self-awareness. They have insight into themselves. How can this be achieved? Modern psychology and classical philosophy can be very useful in our quest for self-insight and the contributions of each may be diligently examined.

A third and supremely effective source of insight is spirituality—a life of faith in and surrender to God and a personal witness flowing from our union with God. The Creator knows what went into the creature and can help us know who we are. Genuine communion with God will grant us insight into our true selves.

The vision of Isaiah in Chapter Six of his book illustrates the connection between experiencing God and coming to a true appreciation of self and what we are called to do. God calls Isaiah to be a prophet. In turn the prophet understands his calling as an act of divine love and compassion. Let us see how his vision discloses for us the connection between the experience of God and growth in self-knowledge.

Born in Jerusalem about the year 762 B.C., Isaiah grew up in a family that trained him to have a sense of justice. His parents educated him to oppose the immoral treatment of the poor by the rich and powerful. They told him about rapacious loan sharks. They showed him how businessmen cheated customers with false weights and measures. They held family discussions about the prevalence of bribery at King Uzziah's court, the corruption of priests and the helplessness of the poor. With them he studied the Bible and absorbed the message of the covenant. His parents gave him a religious and moral conscience which provided a seedbed for the prophetic calling he was about to receive.

On his twenty-first birthday, he received an invitation to the coronation of King Jotham. The ceremony gripped and enchanted him. He listened to the music of the psalms, inhaled the sweet aroma of the incense, was dazzled by the royal procession and the colorful robes of the celebrants—all converging at Solomon's Temple, one of the grandest stages on earth. Clouds of smoke arose from the sacrifices. Deep within the temple, in its third chamber—the Holy of Holies—reposed the Ark of the Covenant.

Suddenly, this physical reality was transposed into a spiritual one, communicating to Isaiah a profound religious experience of God. Angelic music replaced the psalm singers with the acclamation, "Holy, holy, holy is the Lord of hosts. The whole earth is full of his glory."[9] The gold angels kneeling on the Ark of the Covenant changed into real angels, the seraphim whose name means fiery messengers.

The "garments" of God transcended the robes of princes and priests. "The hem of his robe filled the temple."[10] Isaiah felt God as close as cloth against his skin. The incense smoke became the shining biblical cloud which Scripture calls the *shekinah,* a name for the manifest glory of God.

The experience shook Isaiah to his very roots. The earthquake that made the temple tremble was an image of what was going on in Isaiah's soul. "The pivots (foundations) on the threshold shook."[11] Then the vision temporarily faded from his eyes. He had beheld the glory of God and now he was thrown back upon himself where he could compare himself with what he had seen. He was made aware of his own sinfulness when matched with the utter purity of God, of his smallness contrasted with God's majesty, of his helplessness in the face of God's power.

"Woe is me! for I am lost for I am a man of unclean lips...yet my eyes have seen the King, the Lord of hosts."[12] This confession of his nothingness before the transcendence of God was an honest admission of his weaknesses, sins and faults, an evaluation of himself that was prompted by the grace of God who came into his life. It was the moment of his conversion to a life totally dedicated to God.

God proceeded to cleanse and purify him and prepare him for his ministry. A seraph took a live coal from the altar, flew to him, touched his mouth and said, "Now that this has touched your lips, your guilt has departed and your sin is blotted out."[13] This was the fiery anointing of a prophet. God was granting Isaiah the grace of transformation, the gift of purifying union that would make him exquisitely sensitive to God's will for his life and ministry. Love would speak unto love. God had a mission for his new prophet. "Whom shall I send?" Isaiah replied, "Here am I; send me!"[14]

Because Isaiah entered the temple area as a reasonably faithful person and, through God's grace, acquired a deep insight into himself and into the mystery of God, he left the scene as someone who would become one of Israel's greatest prophets. For the next fifty years he witnessed God's holiness and preached the message that people treat one another with simple justice.

Toward the end of his life he realized that no ruler of Israel would really bring justice and holiness to his people.

The advent of a savior was in the future. He began to have visions and dreams of what that savior would be like. This occurred during his "ministry of silence" in the reign of Hezekiah, one of Israel's better kings. Out of that contemplative silence Isaiah produced gorgeous poetic descriptions of what the messiah and his kingdom would be like. That is why so many of his prophecies read like a Christmas Gospel, and Isaiah is a prophet of the Church's liturgical season of Advent.

Isaiah's peak experience of God, the profound conversion that resulted from it and his discovery of a prophetic vocation is a masterful biblical image, in a strikingly dramatic form, of what each of you can experience, most likely at a more subdued and gradual level. I do not deny that you could have the sudden and inspiring kind of change that Isaiah had. Paul's Damascus experience—another famed scriptural example of quick and remarkable change—can also be available to you.

But our history shows that most of us walk the longer road to this joyful union with Christ. For this you have only to read the Gospels which provide you with examples of more gradual conversions in the lives of the apostles. Jesus patiently led Peter and his comrades through a long-term process of faith growth, with many successes and failures until they were ready to receive the great graces of his resurrection and the descent of the Holy Spirit. Whether quick or gradual, the process works by God's graces. God is not contained by any preconceived notions of how to act toward us.

We have been reflecting today on how to walk a humble path. As I read over my journal, I am struck by how often I needed to call myself back to practicing humility. When my closest friend and mentor, Bishop Radini-Tedeschi died, I felt lost and began to fret about my future. I noticed that part of my anxiety was related to ambitious dreams of Church promotions and honors, which now would have to subside because the new bishop would not appoint me to his diocesan leadership family. I had been assigned to the seminary faculty, but I was not yet committed to it. God led me to see these were foolish thoughts, attitudes and desires that had little to do with growth in holiness and virtue. I resolved to put them aside.

> As for fantastic dreams in which my pride may indulge, thoughts of honors, positions, etc., I will be careful not to entertain them, but will spurn them at once. They upset one's peace of mind, sap one's energy, and take all real joy and all value and merit from anything good one may do. For myself I must think only of remaining very humble, very, very humble, leaving everything else to God....
>
> I want to be exemplary in all my professional duties, in my relations with the Rector of the seminary, my colleagues and pupils. I will be very humble and friendly with everyone, doing my best to contribute to the mutual harmony and edification which are so important where such grave responsibilities are shared. Above all, I will refrain from criticizing or complaining about anything and always remember, among other things, that nowhere else could I be so comfortably situated.[15]

I should think you will struggle to walk the humble path just as I did. Do not be discouraged by the difficulties this entails. The journey is well worth the effort. If the very Son of God was willing to do it, you should be filled with joy that you have the same calling. "Jesus, meek and humble of heart, make our hearts like unto thine."

For Reflection

1. Consider pride a blind guide.

The greatest of people tend to be simple and humble and capable of awe. After Adlai Stevenson lost the election to Dwight Eisenhower, he was asked by the outgoing president, Harry Truman, to spend a night at the White House. Truman put the defeated candidate in the Lincoln room. When Stevenson was undressed and ready to retire, he hesitated in awe before the Lincoln bed. He couldn't dream of sleeping in so important a bed. Instead he slept on the sofa. What the great-humble man did not know was: In Lincoln's day, the bed wasn't there. The sofa was.

- *Who are some great (not necessarily famous) people that you know or have met? What do you think makes them great? What can you learn from them?*
- *What stories of humble acts do you remember which inspire you to walk the humble path? List some vanities, foolish dreams or power fantasies you have. How will you let them go?*
- *Who have been the wise mentors in your life? How did they affect your beliefs, attitudes and practices? Who are you mentoring now? How do you help them with the virtue of humility?*

2. Be down to earth.

After his conversion, Saint Augustine assembled a group of young philosophers for a summer seminar on the questions of the day. His mother, Monica, broke in on their proceedings one day and asked how they were doing. Augustine asked the secretary to write down her question. She said, "Why are you doing that? I thought women were not allowed to be part of this discussion." Augustine answered, "You know that philosophy means the love of wisdom. You are the greatest lover of wisdom I have ever met." Just as nimbly she replied, "I have never known you to tell an untruth before."

- *Monica's down-home reply to her son shows us the "earthy" wisdom of the saints. Who are the people you admire most because they are down to earth? How have they affected your behavior?*

- *What are some maxims you use on a regular basis to guide your life? Where did you find them? Which one is your favorite?*

- *Of all the sayings of Jesus, which ones touch you the most? What are some experiences in your life in which these sayings have carried you through a crisis?*

3. Gain insight into yourself.

We have seen in this retreat how Pope John kept a lifelong journal to help him find self-insight. We have heard the story of the religious experience of Isaiah in which he gained an insight into the holiness and justice of God and also his call to prophetic ministry. Meeting God not only shows us who God is, but also tells us a good deal about ourselves.

- *What means do you use to know more about God and more about yourself? What religious experiences have you had throughout your life which brought you closer to Christ and nearer to the "real you"?*

- *What do you notice about people who lack insight about themselves? What lessons do you draw from such observations?*

- *What do you think is the difference between being merely clever and truly wise? What examples from your life illustrate the difference?*

Closing Prayer

To the Child Jesus

O heavenly Child, our almighty Lord, we believe that you grant the requests of those who turn to you with pure hearts and that you also hear the prayers of those who are silent;...

Calm aggressive minds, convert the erring, make your people holy, preserve the purity of virgins, guard the faithfulness of married men and women, fortify the chaste; enlighten those who have only just begun to follow your teaching, and confirm them, make them worthier of loftier attainment, and may we at the last all be eternally reunited in your kingdom, O Jesus, together with you, with the Father and the Holy Spirit, to whom be glory, honour and blessing for ever and ever. Amen.[16]

Notes

[1] *I Will Be Called John*, p. 267.

[2] Ibid.

[3] *Pope John XXIII*, p. 289.

[4] Proverbs 9:1, 2, 4b-6, *NRSV*.

[5] *Pope John XXIII*, p. 47.

[6] *Journal of a Soul*, pp. 431-432.

[7] Alfred McBride, O. Praem., *Saints Are People: Church History Through the Saints* (Dubuque, Iowa: BROWN-ROA, 1981), p. 97.

[8] Ibid., p. 96.

[9] Isaiah 6:3, *NRSV*.

[10] Isaiah 6:1, *NRSV*.

[11] Isaiah 6:4, *NRSV*.

[12] Isaiah 6:5, *NRSV*.

[13] Isaiah 6:7, *NRSV*.

[14] Isaiah 6:8, *NRSV*.

[15] *Journal of a Soul*, pp. 187, 186.
[16] Ibid., p. 377.

Day Five
Love the Church

Coming Together in the Spirit

"I must direct all things, thoughts as well as actions, to the increase, the service and the glory of Holy Church."

On the first Christmas of my papacy, after I celebrated Mass at St. Peter's, I visited the Gesu Bambino children's hospital. This had not been planned, so the nurses and attendants were unsure about what to do. The children had no problem at all. With natural and unrestrained enthusiasm they shouted, "Papa, Papa, come over here to us."

I replied, "Quiet now, I'm coming to see all of you."

I made my way from bed to bed and talked with the children. One little boy told me his name was Angelo. I told him that was my name too. I sat for a long time by the side of a child who had lost his sight. I held his hand and said, "We are all blind sometimes, my dear child. Perhaps it will be given to you to see more than others."[1]

My visits outside the Vatican, such as this one, were rare. My major contact with large groups of people was in the weekly audiences. One of my first audiences was held in the Clementine Hall for the hundreds of journalists from around the world who had come to cover the papal election and the coronation. I acknowledged the great power of the press: "Even in numbers you resemble an army." I also noted the distinction and importance of their calling.

I teased them about their efforts to guess what went on in the conclave. "One newspaper even purported to give an hour-by-hour account of what went on in the conclave, and do you know,...there were not two lines of truth in the whole thing!... You write about a political pope, a scholarly pope, a diplomatic pope. But the fact is that the pope is simply the pope, the 'good shepherd' who looks for ways to bring souls to truth. 'Truth and goodness' are his two wings. No one should construct a pope according to any other ideas, especially not a private one.... Now I will give you a small blessing, if you wish to receive it. And this blessing will carry to all who are dear to you."[2]

Defining Our Thematic Context

Wise People Walk a Humble Path

Self-important people are very proud of what they know. Wise people are humble because they know what they do not know. In our retreat we are making the case for wisdom and have seen how love, simplicity and serenity contribute to this virtue. On Day Four we considered humility's connection with wisdom. I invited you to focus on these three points: (1) Consider pride a blind guide. (2) Be down to earth. (3) Gain insight into yourself. Today we see how love for the Church as our mother and teacher is another pillar of wisdom.

Opening Prayer

Holy Spirit of wisdom,

teach us how to love the Church.
Show us her role as mother and teacher,
a mother who begets us in Christ through the
sacraments,
a teacher who holds Christ ever before us,
a mother who loves us with genuine affection,
a teacher who guides us to heaven,
a mother who prays for our needs,
a teacher who shows us the meaning of Christ.
Jesus, incarnate wisdom, reveal to us
the mystery of Church as your Body.
Give us the love we need to be in the Church
as a communion of love.
Deepen our faith in the Church
as the sacrament of salvation
and the light of nations.
Help us love the Church.

Retreat Session Five

Rebuild My Church

One day as Saint Francis of Assisi was praying before the lovely Cross of San Damiano, he heard Jesus say from the Cross, "Francis, rebuild my Church." I applied those words to myself when I became, at seventy-two, the patriarch of Venice. I have always tried to love the Church in the spirit of Saint Paul's words to the Ephesians. "Christ loved the church and gave himself up for her, in order to make her holy...so as to present the church to himself in splendor, without spot or wrinkle or anything of the kind."[3]

For the first time in my life I was able to act as a pastor and get involved in rebuilding the Church both materially and spiritually. During my five-year patriarchate I established thirty new parishes, built a minor seminary and ordered some major renovations of the cathedral. I ordered the restoration of the burial crypt beneath the altar of the cathedral. The tomb of Saint Mark was raised so it could be visible for veneration.

Behind St. Mark's stood a row of church buildings, in serious disrepair, where the aged canons of the cathedral lived. I wanted them repaired and restored, but the chairman of the committee told me the old men would not move while the work went on. I went to see them myself and returned to tell the chairman that everything was arranged. "But what did you say, eminence?" "The same thing you did, my dear friend, but I kept in mind that all these good fathers were all past seventy years of age and a little frightened of having to leave their home, even for a little while. And so I said it in a softer way."

Vincent Auriol, the former president of France and a good friend of mine from my days as nuncio to Paris, came to visit me. People were fascinated that I could have a warm friendship with this socialist nonbeliever, but we had discovered a common humanity which tied us together. I was showing him around the palace when I brought him to a modest, poorly furnished little room. I said, "Here lived Pius X." And then I found I couldn't say any more; I was so overcome with emotion. He had blessed me the day after my ordination over fifty years before and the memory overtook me. Auriol honored my silence.

I did not always get what I wanted. There was a marble screen in front of the altar of St. Mark's, which obscured it from the view of the worshipers. I believed the time had come for all the faithful to see the altar and participate in the liturgy. I talked with various committees, the mayor, the fine arts commission, but nothing was done.

Then I proposed that, rather than remove the masterpiece, it be mounted on pivots, so it could be wheeled aside during Mass, and then returned to its place. People criticized me, saying tourists taking pictures would profane the sanctuary. I mildly replied, "Is St. Peter's altar profaned? Millions come every year and gaze in awe at the altar." Still nothing happened.

A few months after I became pope, I said to a visiting Venetian, "About that marble screen...." In a few weeks, it was mounted just as I suggested, and there was nothing but praise for the change.

It takes a lot of wisdom to be a good pastor. One source of this wisdom is love for the Church in all its many manifestations, as an organization, a community of believers, the Body of Christ, the people of God and a sacrament of salvation. The genius of wisdom is that it sees the whole picture and all its parts.

Wisdom has the capacity to think of many matters at one time, yet never lose the potential unity underneath all this variety. Wisdom can even hold apparent contradictions together—such as the humanity and divinity of Jesus, the Church as organization and community, the importance of law and the sanctity of freedom—and never get flustered or confused.

I have proposed to you some of the pillars upon which wisdom is built: love, simplicity, serenity and humility. Now I want to share with you another pillar of wisdom: love for the Church. Here are some basic elements which contribute to this love.

1. Commit yourself to the Church as a communion of love.

I have to admit, and am sorry to say so, that too many people look at the Church only in terms of its visible organization. Some consider the Church as a service station to take care of needs like baptisms, weddings and funerals. I heard someone characterize the Church as a place where one goes to be "hatched, matched and dispatched." Seen this way, the Church has become a problem for many people because they find the institution impersonal, unfeeling, unresponsive.

The emphasis on the Church as a visible institution goes back to the sixteenth-century Counter-Reformation in which the Church needed a powerful exposition of its visible aspect to counter the Protestants' exclusive attention to the invisible side of the Church. Saint Robert Bellarmine expressed our position tersely in a legal, external manner: "It (the Church) is the perfect, visible society of those who are baptized, profess the same faith, celebrate the same sacraments, and are united under the jurisdiction of the Roman Pontiff."

This is not to say that there was no appreciation of the spiritual quality of the Church and its invisible mystery throughout all these centuries. Millions of holy people and saints were bred by the grace of the Holy Spirit through the ministry of the Church year after year. But in our day it became clear a change—call it a course correction—was needed.

Related to this, I have watched with interest the growth of the liturgical movement and the writings of the theologians of the French school, especially Henri de Lubac, Yves Congar and Jean Danielou. They went back to the writings of the Fathers of the Church where they uncovered the rich teachings about the communal, mystical and sacramental quality of the Church. Pope Pius

XII moved in a similar direction in his ground-breaking encyclical, *Mystici Corporis* ("Mystical Body").

The fruits of their labors were already apparent to me at the first session of Vatican II. The first of the seventy-two documents the Council dealt with was titled, *De Ecclesia Christi Militante* ("The Militant Church of Christ"). It described the Church in visible, legal, institutional terms. On the floor of the Council one bishop after another stood up and criticized the document as triumphalistic, clericalistic and legalistic. One bishop, lamenting the futile energy put into the document, said, quoting the Gospel, "We have worked all night long and have caught nothing."[4]

The Fathers wanted a new document with a richer approach. This was achieved under my successor, Pope Paul VI, and expressed in the Council document, *Lumen Gentium* ("Light of Nations"). Now we had a teaching which explored the full reality of the Church, its invisible side as mystery, Body of Christ, Temple of the Holy Spirit, People of God, Sacrament of Salvation and a Communion of the Members in Christ by the power of the Spirit. At the same time, its visible, hierarchical structure was also included.

These fresh insights into the meaning of the Church, already basically present in the writings of the Fathers and in the research of many theologians in the years preceding the Council, are vital sources for our spiritual reflection in this retreat. The images of the Church as People of God and Communion in the Spirit pertain to the point I wish to dwell on here.

The Holy Trinity is the original community of love. Our heavenly Father, in an act of pure freedom, goodness and wisdom, created the whole universe and chose to raise us men and women up to share in his divine life, calling us to communion in his divine Son. Our heavenly Father called together in our holy Church all those who would believe in Christ. This family of God was gradually formed and took shape in history and was prepared for in the life of the people of Israel and the first covenant.

Then the Church was established by Jesus in this final era of world history, made manifest at Pentecost through the outpouring of the Spirit, and it will be brought to glorious completion at the end of time. From this brief outline you can see the panorama of the Trinity's activity toward and absolute interest in the shaping of our Church. The loving communion of the Trinity thus finds an earthly echo in the loving communion of the People of God in the Church.

When meditating on this intimate connection between the Church and the action of the Trinity, I urge you to adopt this motto, "Become who you are." In other words, become the loving community of brothers and sisters in Christ and the Spirit, whom you have been made by your baptism, the gift of faith and the life of the sacraments, especially the Eucharist.

The Fathers of the Church loved to call the Church the Body of Christ, the same name as that given to the Eucharist. They also said that the Body of Christ in the Eucharist is meant to build up the Body of Christ in the Church. Hence the Church's growth flows from the divine love in the sacrament into our lives, which we then share with each other and with the world through acts of love, justice and mercy.

Perhaps now you can see why I ask you to love the Church which is both the means and the goal of salvation. In loving the Church you are both loving one another and the Father, Son and Spirit who dwell in the Church's heart.

When I wrote my first encyclical on social justice, I entitled it *Mater et Magistra* ("Mother and Teacher"). I had seen this phrase in Pope Innocent III's address to the fourth Lateran Council (1215), and I bring it to your attention in this context. I see our Church as a loving mother who gives birth to us in Christ and nourishes us with the sacraments. I see her as a teacher who ministers to our basic hunger for God and for the truth by her teaching ministry. My mother and teacher is always feeding me with the Word of God and the Bread of God at the table of the Word and the Table of the Sacrament. With so much love coming to me, what else can I do but graciously return this love? Treasure these truths in your minds and devote your meditations to this precious gift from God. Love the Church.

2. Appreciate the mystery of the Church.

Sometimes I have experienced the mystery of the Church in painful ways before penetrating its overwhelming beauty. A good example of this was the morning I announced the calling of an ecumenical council on January 25, 1959, the feast of the conversion of Saint Paul. I was up before dawn as usual, offered Mass and stayed in the chapel until 9:30. After breakfast a car was waiting for me to take me to the basilica of St. Paul's. I was uncharacteristically silent and news photos of my arrival showed me to be anxious and tense. I worried about how the cardinals would accept my announcement.

After the prayer service in the basilica, precisely at 1:00 p.m., the seventeen cardinals made their way into the chapter room of the Benedictine abbey (the Benedictines had charge of the basilica). My talk began at 1:10 and lasted a half hour. I opened my heart to them, trusting in their goodness and understanding. I tactfully admitted that my first three months in the papacy was that of a newcomer to the ways of the Vatican. I noted how Rome had changed since my student days. The cardinals listened attentively but sat there impassively. I spoke briefly about the Church's presence in a world with many problems.

Toward the end of my talk, I told them I had reached a decision. I was following a tradition in which the Church sought greater clarity of thought, the strengthening of the bond of unity and a greater spiritual fervor.

> Venerable brothers and our beloved sons! Trembling with emotion, and yet with humble resolution, we put before you the proposal of a double celebration: a diocesan synod for Rome and an ecumenical council for the universal Church.... [I ask you to pray for] a good start, a successful implementation and a happy outcome for those projects which will involve hard work for the enlightenment, the edification and the joy of the Christian people,...[5]

The seventeen cardinals responded to my speech and announcement with silence. No applause. No one getting up and speaking out in joyful support of the plan. I was very disappointed.

> Humanly speaking, we would have expected that the cardinals, after listening to our address, might have crowded round to express their approval and good wishes.... It's not a matter of my personal feelings. We are embarked on the will of the Lord.... Now I need silence and recollection. I feel tired of everyone, of everything.[6]

There I was with the major leaders of the Curia and receiving so puzzling a response. I later tried to put the best interpretation on it, saying the idea must have stunned them into silence! But my faith was tested and I experienced the mystery of the Church in its darkness rather than its light.

Why do we speak of the Church as mystery? First, because the Church had a divine founder, as already mentioned above in my discussion of the relation of Trinity to Church. The Father intended and planned for the Church when the world was created. The Son of God, Jesus Christ, established the Church. The Holy Spirit visibly manifested the Church at Pentecost. This means the Church is not created by the consent of the members, but is a gift from the Holy Trinity which lovingly calls us into the community of the Church.

Second, the Church is mystery because the Holy Spirit is the enduring, cohesive force, maintaining the stability and continuity of the Church. While our human effort and perseverance is necessary in this task, our determination alone is not enough. We need the power of the Spirit, not just human forcefulness. The Spirit holds the Church together no matter if the historical and sociological occurrences are favorable or unfavorable. The Spirit sustained the existence of the Church during the Roman persecutions as well as during the glory days of the high Middle Ages.

Third, the Church is mystery because of the divine life and salvation that comes to us in the sacraments. We are not saving ourselves. Only God can save us. We call the Church the sacrament of salvation, not just because it points to Christ's saving work, but also because it contains and produces this salvation.

No purely human explanation can fully account for the mystery of the Church, though historical and archaeological studies make genuine contributions to understanding the human aspects of the Church's emergence and development. Only religious faith can perceive the divine Trinitarian plan at work in the incredible history of the Church. The Church is in history, but at the same time, transcends it. Faith helps us see her visible reality and at the same time her invisible spiritual reality as the bearer of divine life. The Church is simultaneously a visible society and a spiritual community, an earthly institution and a reality endowed with heavenly riches.

With his customary poetic flair, Saint Bernard says this of the Church:

> O humility! O sublimity!
> Both tabernacle of cedar and sanctuary of God
> Earthly dwelling and celestial palace
> House of clay and royal hall
> Body of death and temple of light
> And at last both object of scorn to the proud
> and bride of Christ![7]

The lives of the saints and the millions of quietly devout Catholics are yet another testimony to the mystery of the Church. These "miracles of grace" have existed in every age of the Church and do so today. Is this not why you are making this retreat? Are you not seeking to make the mystery of the Church a living reality in your lives? Are you not reaching out for the beyond to come into your midst? Is not your faith but an act of seeking to understand and live the mystery of Christ manifest in the Church which is his Body and the Temple of the Holy Spirit?

Appreciate the mystery of the Church. Wisdom will help you hold together the divine and human sides of the mystery without getting confused or yielding to the temptation to just look at one side and forget the other.

3. Recognize the Church as a sacrament.

The Church is the sacrament of salvation, pointing to, containing and producing, by the power of Holy Spirit, the saving work of Jesus Christ. A sacrament is an effective sign, instituted by Christ, entrusted to the Church, to give us divine life. A sacrament is composed of visible and invisible elements. A sacrament is a visible, tangible reality used to convey God's invisible life and grace to us.

Why do we have sacraments? Because they are related to our human condition, composites of body and soul. The Greek philosophers said, "Nothing is in the mind that does not first come through the senses." As human beings we must go through something we can see and feel if we hope to get in touch with the supernatural. This is the earthy realism of the Church and the sacraments.

Once you have accepted this you can understand that the primary sacrament is Jesus himself. He is the visible sign and presence of God in the world. "He is the image of the invisible God" (Colossians 1:15). Through his human nature we encounter God. Jesus is the chief sacrament and sign of God for us. "All this is from God who reconciled us to himself through Christ...in Christ God was reconciling the world to himself."[8]

Now that Jesus has risen from the dead and ascended into heaven, he can no longer be visibly present to us as he was in Galilee and Judea. Jesus is now present to us in the Church and in the Holy Eucharist and the other sacraments. For our purpose here, the Church has become the sacrament of our inner union with God. Because our communion with one another is rooted in this union with God, the Church is also the sacrament of the union of the human race. This unity has already begun for the Church has gathered to her heart people "from every nation, from all tribes and peoples and languages" (Revelation 7:9). At the same time the Church is the sign and instrument of the full realization that is yet to come.

From my vantage point as pope I have had many experiences of the Church as a gathering place for the world. In St. Peter's Square the circular arms of Bernini's collonade seem to embrace the hundreds of thousands who come each year to see the pope and the great basilica. When I see the throngs in the square I behold the present unity within the Church and the possible unity for the world that lies ahead. Of course, I am not blind to the divisions within the Church or among the churches nor between Christianity and the world. If I had not noticed that I would never have called a council. But my temperament is to look at where unity exists and then work to bring others into that blessed communion.

Let me tell you a story which will more easily help you to see why the Church must be a sacrament of salvation. In 1523 a young Florentine painter brought his masterpiece, "The Bark of Peter," done in oils, to Pope Adrian VI.

> His bark was carried by angels blowing eschatological trumpets. The waters beneath the ship were calm, but all around, the waves were whipped up in fury and full of drowning sinners, heretics, and schismatics. The Pope sat on the deck of this bark, eyes closed, hands clasped in prayer, surrounded by his Curia, his household, and his guards, while the faces of the faithful peeped out of the square portholes below. The sails were limp and white and the papal yellow stood straight out from the masts. The rudder was raised out of the water, and around it three figures read a Bible opened to the illuminated words "Thou art Peter; and upon this rock..."
>
> Adrian (who was a Dutchman,...) cried out at this monstrosity, "No, no, this is not my ship, this is not my ship." The startled painter hastened to explain. "This is the bark of Peter," he said, "high above the stormy seas of heresy, preserved from contamination by the angels of light." "No, my son," replied Adrian, "you do not understand. Perhaps we ourselves have understood only lately. The dimensions are wrong." The painter's patron, a rich

> Florentine merchant, broke in and told Adrian respectfully that the Master, Giacomo, had trained the lad and really ought to know what the dimensions should be. Adrian answered sadly: "No. No. Put my ship upon these troubled waters. Fill the sails and dip the rudder in the sea and let me steer my bishops and their flocks. We must calm the waters and be saved with these." He knocked his fisherman's ring against the writhing figures in the water. "And these, and these, and these."[9]

How well this wonderful story describes how the Church should be a sacrament of salvation. It reflects the spirit of Christ's command to go and seek the lost sheep. It recovers Christ's tears about Jerusalem and his dismay that, in his time, there were so many sheep without a shepherd. A Church that would forget its mission to save people would be like the ship in this picture.

When I think of the Church as the sign of the unity between us and God and of the potential unity of the whole human race, I think back to the evening of October 10, 1962. Five hundred thousand people had jammed into St. Peter's Square for a torchlight demonstration of their joy about the council which was to open the next day. Recall that forty-five months earlier I bore a deep disappointment when I announced the council. Now I felt as though the whole world had come, with hope and enthusiasm, to open the council.

I said to them, "Dear children, dear children, I hear your voices. My voice is an isolated one, but it echoes the voice of the whole world. Here, in effect, the whole world is represented." I was emotionally overwhelmed by the size and enthusiasm of the crowd, their shouts, their torches, and the light of a rose-colored moon, which, I pointed out to them, was "also contemplating this spectacle."

On that unforgettable Roman evening, the vigil of the feast of the Motherhood of God, a celebration that recalled an earlier council of the Church, Ephesus in 431, I knew I had made the right decision. "The glow and sweetness of the Lord takes hold of us and unites us."[10]

Love for the Church will motivate you to create a loving communion of believers, united by the Holy Spirit, devoted to Jesus and embarked on a journey to the Father. It will inspire you to have an affection for all the people of the world with whom you wish to share the immense range of gifts available to you from the Church and the sacraments. Love for the Church will draw you to study its history, ponder the lives of its saints and increase your understanding of the marvel of the gift we have received from the Holy Trinity. Love for the Church will expand your sensitivity to the needs of the poor, the vocation to establish justice and peace in your community and the world itself. Reverence for the mystery of the Church will touch your faith and make it purer and put you in touch with the giver of wisdom, the virtue to which I ask you to aspire.

For Reflection

1. Commit yourself to the Church as a communion of love.

> [T]he New Testament gives the name *body of Christ*,...to three realities, each linked with the others: the fleshly body born of Mary,...the Eucharistic and sacramental body; the community or Church-body of which the faithful are the members. It is not without purpose and reason that these three realities have the same name: the body of Christ. They are genuinely linked one to another, since the first takes the form of

> the second so that it may exist in the third. There is only one spiritual temple, the body of Christ, but this body now glorified exists on earth in the Church, which is the spiritual temple and the house of God.[11]

Good theology leads to sound spirituality. Spend some time meditating on this passage from Congar. Bring the thoughts to your mind and heart in prayer.

- *Why is the formation of a loving communion of Christians the expected outcome of the Church as communion and body of Christ?*
- *What can you do to strengthen the Church as communion in your family, your parish, your neighborhood?*

2. Appreciate the mystery of the Church.

> The Church grows from the inside outwards, not the other way round. What it means above all is the most inward community with Christ: it takes shape in the life of prayer, in the life of the sacraments; in the fundamental attitudes of faith, hope and love. If therefore someone asks: "What must I do so that the Church may come into being and progress?" the answer must be: "What you must strive for above all is for faith to exist, for people to hope and to love." Prayer builds the Church and the community of the sacraments, in which its prayer reaches us.[12]

- *How would you help someone appreciate the Church as mystery? Why would you speak of prayer, reverence and divine presence when discoursing about the Church?*
- *If we only try to build up our Church from the outside in, instead of from the inside out, what could we expect?*
- *What experiences have you had of the inward nature of the Church? What would open you to this in the future?*

3. Recognize the Church as a sacrament.

> In contemporary ecclesiology the concept of sacrament is prominent. A sacrament, according to the traditional understanding, is a visible sign of an invisible grace. It contains and transmits the grace that it signifies. All these characteristics of sacrament are preeminently verified in Christ, and, after him, in the Church. Christ is the sacrament of God.... The Church, in turn, is the sacrament of Christ.[13]

- *Granting the Church is the sacrament of salvation, how often have you been willing to share your faith in Christ and the Church with others? How do you do it?*
- *What do you think needs to be done to attract more people to experience the joy of salvation brought by the Church?*
- *How is your spiritual life enhanced by the gift of the Church as the sacrament of salvation?*

Closing Prayer

Father, I thank you for intending and planning the Church. Son, I praise you for establishing the Church. Holy Spirit, I adore you for making the Church manifest at Pentecost and for abiding with the Church ever since. Give me the daily grace to appreciate the Church as a communion of love, a mystery of God and a sacrament of salvation. Teach me how to live these great truths about the Church, to grow in love for her and to share my faith with others. Amen.

Notes

[1] *I Will Be Called John*, p. 271.

[2] Ibid., p. 273.

[3] Ephesians 5:25-27, *NRSV*.

[4] Luke 5:5, *NRSV*.

[5] *Pope John XXIII*, p. 321.

[6] Ibid., p. 322.

[7] Sermon on the Song of Songs, 27:14, by Saint Bernard of Clairvaux.

[8] 2 Corinthians 5:18-19, *NRSV*.

[9] Robert Blair Kaiser, *Pope, Council and World: The Story of Vatican II* (New York: The Macmillan Company, 1963), p. 2.

[10] Ibid., p. 91.

[11] Yves M.-J. Congar, O.P., *The Mystery of the Temple OR The Manner of God's Presence to His Creatures from Genesis to the Apocalypse*, trans. Reginald F. Trevett (Westminster, Md.: The Newman Press, 1962) p. 189.

[12] Cardinal Joseph Ratzinger, *Church, Ecumenism and Politics: New Essays in Ecclesiology* (New York: Crossroad, 1988), p. 5.

[13] Avery Dulles, S.J., *A Church to Believe In: Discipleship and the Dynamics of Freedom* (New York: Crossroad, 1982), p. 46.

Day Six

Make Me an Instrument of Your Peace

Coming Together in the Spirit

"I beg the heads of state not to remain insensitive to the cry of humanity: Peace! Peace!"

On October 20, 1962, just eight days after the opening of the council, President John F. Kennedy announced the blockade of Cuba, effectively barring Russian ships making for that country. The Cuban Missile Crisis had begun. In Rio de Janeiro, Dr. Billy Graham announced the end of the world, prematurely as it turned out, but not unreasonably. Civilization was face to face with nuclear catastrophe.

Just a year before I had received a birthday greeting from Chairman Krushchev. I promptly sent a note of thanks and added, "I will pray for the people of Russia." I had also assured the Soviet government that there would not be an attack against communism on the council agenda. Krushchev was doubtless puzzled by a pope who did not parade a militant anti-communism. One effect of these conciliatory overtures was the permission for two representatives of the Russian Orthodox Church to be observers at the council.

Now in the midst of the missile crisis I wanted to

speak out for the world and beg for peace. I hoped I could mediate between Krushchev and Kennedy. Providentially, the influential editor of the *Saturday Review,* Norman Cousins, learned of my willingness to appeal for peace if it would help the antagonists pull away from the brink. Cousins conveyed this message to the White House and the Kremlin. The president and the chairman agreed this would be a step in the search for peace.

On October 26, 1962, I sat before a sea of radio microphones and, in French, appealed for peace. "Hear the anguished cry which rises to heaven from every corner of the earth, from innocent children to old men, from the people in cities and villages: Peace! Peace!" The world's newspapers, including those in Russia, headlined my message. The tension eased. Two days later Krushchev announced that Russian missiles would be withdrawn from Cuba. President Kennedy praised the chairman for his statesmanship.

Cousins followed up the move to peace by going to Moscow to press Kennedy's proposal for a nuclear test ban. Cousins also told the chairman about my hope for religious liberty in Russia for all believers and my desire for the release of Archbishop Slipyi, imprisoned since 1944 when charged by Stalin with Nazi collaboration.

Then Cousins came to see me. I put him at ease, "We have much to talk about. I'm an ordinary man. I have two eyes, a nose—a very large nose. You must feel completely relaxed." I gave Cousins a papal medal. I told him I had a second one for anyone Cousins would recommend. I was hinting, without saying so, that I would like to give it to Krushchev. A few weeks later, Slipyi was released and sent to Rome. I sent the second medal to Krushchev. I am told he keeps it on his desk at all times. When visitors come in, he plays with it. He lures them into asking about it and then says, "Oh, it's only a medal from the pope."[1]

Defining Our Thematic Context

Wise People Make Peace

In our retreat we have explored various paths to wisdom including: the need for love, simplicity of life, inner calm, a humble approach to life and love for the Church. These are conditions for the possibility of receiving wisdom from God. Ultimately wisdom is like breath coming from God, an emanation of the divine glory. Scripture tells us this about wisdom:

> [Wisdom] is a breath of the power of God, and a pure emanation of the glory of the Almighty. She is a reflection of eternal light; a spotless mirror of the working of God, and an image of his goodness.... For (wisdom) is more beautiful than the sun, and excels every constellation of the stars.... I became enamored of her beauty.[2]

In our last meditation we pondered the value of loving the Church as a route to wisdom. I asked you to think of these points: (1) Commit yourself to the Church as a communion of love. (2) Appreciate the mystery of the Church. (3) Recognize the Church as a sacrament.

Our next consideration of the sources of wisdom is the quest for peace. I invite you to assimilate the beautiful words of Saint Francis, "Lord, make me an instrument of your peace." Let us pray for this gift.

Opening Prayer

Risen Lord, on Easter night, your first words
to the apostles were, "Peace be with you."
You emphasized the importance of this greeting
by repeating it once again, "Peace be with you."
Your death and resurrection established peace

between God and the people of the world.
You made this reconciliation possible between
us and God and among ourselves and within
ourselves.

In the Sacrament of Reconciliation you offer us
shalom—peace—the forgiveness of our sins.
Thus we are reconciled to you, to the Church—
and to ourselves.
Move us to accept your divine acceptance
so that we might become your ministers of
peace to our families, friends, communities
and even to the world itself.

RETREAT SESSION SIX

Unify People

The word "devil" means discord. Satan is happy when he can sow divisions among families, communities and nations. Jesus stands for love, friendliness and community. Jesus rejoices when we have healed a relationship, restored a friendship, brought peace to a family and done our part in keeping the world at peace.

I thanked God for the resolution of the missile crisis but believed I had a final call to contribute to world peace. It was not easy. I was entering my eighty-second year, battling a painful cancer and trying to keep the first session of the council on track. I decided to write my farewell encyclical, *Pacem in Terris* ("Peace on Earth").

The successful conclusion of the first session of the council, December 8, 1962, gave me a new burst of energy. The reception of the Balzan Peace Prize strengthened my resolve to go ahead with the encyclical. And being chosen as *Time*'s "Man of the Year," (another outcome of Norman Cousins' advocacy) convinced me more than ever I had what your generation calls a "window of oportunity." The magazine noted that "To the entire world Pope John has given what neither diplomacy nor science could give: a sense of the unity of the human family."[3]

In February Time-Life invited me to a unique luncheon in New York City, where other guests would include Kennedy, Krushchev, Charles de Gaulle, Konrad Adenauer, Karl Barth and Pablo Picasso—all of whom had made *Time*'s cover. I did not reject the idea out of hand, but I believed it needed more time to mature. It showed me, however, how effective the Holy See could be in helping the world seek peace. We could be partners with all people of goodwill in the quest of unifying people. President Kennedy was coming to see me in May. Meanwhile, I began the encyclical which I finished in Lent and published on Holy Thursday.

Still, dear friends, our retreat is not meant to dwell on international affairs per se. We are engaged in the search for interior wisdom emanating from the divine glory. Our first task is personal conversion to Christ who is incarnate wisdom. Personal conversion is an absolute prerequisite for active ministry. I could never have had the courage or strength to speak out for peace unless I had spent many years and long hours in prayer and repentance. I needed to be conformed to the wisdom of Jesus before I would have the insight and the daring to invite the world to choose peace rather than conflict.

The effectiveness of public action is in direct proportion to the depth of our inner lives. Unless my soul was filled with wisdom I would have nothing wise to say or do. Every day I say, "Bless the Lord, my soul and let all that is within me praise Christ's holy name." I attribute everything to Jesus and to the powerful intercession of our Blessed Mother to whom I have had a lifelong, steadfast devotion. There is no other way. And to a pragmatic world, I gently insist, this is the most practical approach of all.

We have reviewed five pillars of wisdom: love, simplicity, serenity, humility and affection for the Church. Now let us dwell on the sixth foundation of wisdom—becoming an instrument of Christ's peace.

1. Bring order to your inner life.

From my earliest days in the seminary as a very young man, I was acutely concerned about preserving my celibacy and acquiring the virtue of chastity. I was circumspect about my relations with women. I occasionally went overboard, but was not this an expected step toward spiritual equilibrium, a balancing act, that is characteristic of a young person trying to aquire any desired virtue?

I thought I was doing rather well when suddenly I was faced with raw temptations and a slice of life that I had been protected from in my childhood home and seminary environment. At the end of my first year at the Roman seminary, at age twenty, I was inducted into the army for a year of compulsory military service, as was customary for all men of my age. I became Private Roncalli, of the 73rd Infantry Regiment, the Lombardy Brigade, stationed at Bergamo.

In many ways I fared rather well in the army. I was promoted to corporal in May 1902 and sergeant in November. Believe it or not, I scored high marks on the rifle range. I even managed to get arrested and confined to barracks during the summer maneuvers, mainly because my men proved insubordinate. All during the year the colonel treated me with respect and allowed me the fullest liberty to pursue my religious practices.

On the darker side I was unprepared for the barracks talk and the boasting about sexual conquests by the soldiers. I wanted my soul to be a mirror reflecting the purity of the angels, of Mary and Jesus. Army life gave me another vision, which I judged quite harshly.

> O the world is so ugly, filthy and loathesome! In my year of military service I have learnt all about it. The army is a running fountain of pollution, enough to submerge whole cities. Who can hope to escape from this flood of slime, unless God comes to his aid?
>
> I thank you, my God, for having preserved me from so much corruption. This has really been one of your noblest gifts, for which I shall be grateful my whole life long.
>
> I did not think a reasonable man could fall so low. Yet it is a fact. Today, after my brief experience, I think it is true to say that more than half of all mankind, at some time in their lives, become animals, without shame. And the priests? O God, I tremble when I think that not a few, even among these, betray their sacred calling.[4]

One of the risks of keeping a diary, as this passage illustrates, is the retention of embarrassingly severe judgments. These were the words of a very serious seminarian, no joking, and somewhat inclined to priggishness. On the positive side I am reminded of how powerful God's grace was in me, preserving my chastity and commitment to celibacy.

Just twelve years later, in World War I, I was back in the army as a chaplain for the duration. I was older and wiser and far more sympathetic then to the troops, mostly peasant conscripts caught up in a conflict they did not understand. Once again I became a sergeant. I no longer saw the army as a sink of iniquity. I came to know the men and appreciate their unnoticed qualities. With some patience and the grace of God I was able to win many of them over to faith and to set aside their anti-clericalism which was mostly superficial.

My work in the army hospital put me in touch with many soldiers of great integrity. I recall 19-year-old Orazi Domenico, struggling with pneumonia. He was a humble peasant with the soul of an angel. He said to me, "For me, Father, to die now would be a blessing: I would willingly die because I feel that by the grace of God my soul still remains innocent.... I'd like to die now, Father, with you beside me, so that I can remain completely the Lord's until my last breath."[5]

To my great sorrow, one month later, he died suddenly, while undergoing an operation.

I cite my two experiences with military life, partly because they remind me of the dreadful costs of war, a memory that was with me when I wrote *Pacem in Terris.* But I also remember them because they marked stages in my inner struggle to control the disorder of my passions. I clearly had more maturity by the time I became a chaplain in World War I, hence I was less rash and more compassionate in judging the weaknesses of others.

Nevertheless, throughout my life I took to heart the advice of Saint Paul. "For this is the will of God, your sanctification: that you abstain from fornication, that each one of you know how to control your own body in holiness and honor.... For God did not call us to impurity but to holiness. Therefore, whoever rejects this rejects not human authority but God who also gives his Holy Spirit to you."[6]

The knowledge that God gives us the Spirit to accomplish within us the ordering of our inner lives has always been consoling to me. It is a sign of God's sympathy for he knows how difficult our struggle is. How marvelously then does he fill us with the Spirit's power to achieve inner harmony.

My own experience has shown me that order inside is helped by order in our outer lives. I have been faithful all my life to a set of little rules which govern my external behavior, rules about set times for prayer, regular self-examination and confession, weekly, monthly and annual reviews of my spiritual state. Discipline on the outside assists inner discipline.

Cardinal Newman understood the role of habits in this regard.

> Nothing is more difficult than to be disciplined and regular in our religion. It is very easy to be religious by fits and starts, and to keep up our feelings by artificial stimulants; but regularity seems to trammel us, and we become impatient.... We do not know what we mean by a habit, except as a state or quality of mind under which we act in this or that particular way; it is a permanent power in the mind.... We have power over our deeds...we have no direct power over our habits. Let us but secure our actions...and our habits will follow.[7]

However, this is not the whole story. I am not reducing spirituality to a regimen of piety, a list of spiritual practices, which, if done daily and strictly on a timely basis, will yield interior order and personal holiness. I certainly believe in the importance of repeated acts that induce habits which lead to inner order and outward stability.

But I also advocate a personal relationship with God, Father, Son and Spirit, along with personal devotion to Mary and the saints. I take seriously the beautiful words of the two disciples on the Emmaus Road, "Were not our hearts burning within us while he was talking to us on the road, while he was opening up the scriptures to us?"[8]

Jesus personally came into their lives in the midst of their sorrows, questions and despair. He encouraged them to share their experiences with him and brought out their questions. They had been focusing on Jesus and he came into their midst, a wonderful application of his own teaching that where two or three are gathered in his name, he would come to them.

You might say that Jesus formed them into a small community with himself, opened their minds to his teachings and touched their hearts with his love. As this personal relationship blossomed around the heartfelt experience of Jesus and his life-giving word, they are led to the table of the Eucharist where they break the Bread with him and recognize his risen presence.

If you have the opportunity and inclination to read my *Journal of a Soul*, you will find numerous instances of how I was led by grace into a loving, personal communion with Jesus.

> Jesus, here I am once more this year, in your presence, to listen to your divine teaching. I long to consecrate myself with all solemnity to you, once and for all. The Church has called me; you invite me: "Lo, I come." I have no pretensions, I have no preconceived plans, I am trying to strip myself of all that is self, I am no longer my own. My soul is open before you, like a blank sheet of paper. Write on it what you will, O Lord: I am yours.[9]

I ask you to consider the role of regular spiritual exercises in your quest for inner order, but these are only means to an end, which is a living, vital and warm-hearted relationship with Jesus, the Holy Trinity, Mary, the angels and the saints. The rules and habits are conditions for the possibility of this relationship.

Of course, you must always remember the role of

grace, the fruitful action of the Holy Spirit in all of this. We are considering here a life of faith. I have been emphasizing your responsibilities in the area of religious acts and habits and your striving to reach God personally, and I know that may weigh heavy upon you, necessary though it be. At the same time you must be confident that the Holy Spirit is living and active in this process you experience. Jesus says this yoke is easy and the burden is light. It is grace that makes it so. It is the Spirit who warms the rules and habits into a fire of love that makes the relationship have an effortless feeling to it.

When I introduced this section about inner order, I used examples from my life about the quest for chastity and spoke of disordered passions. Let me refine this a little further.

Disordered passions include more than lust; they embrace what are called the capital sins: anger, pride, envy, sloth, gluttony and greed. I assure you I needed to work on controlling these disorderly drives within me just as much as that which would assail my celibacy. I mentioned earlier in the retreat how often I needed to temper my anger when I saw my subordinates being insensitive to others. But let us proceed to another issue in our quest to be instruments of Christ's peace.

2. Be a peacemaker.

When I was Patriarch of Venice I had to deal with the presence of the communists and the relaxed moral atmophere in the Lido where international film festivals were held. I said nothing about the Lido. I did not give the communists any opportunity to criticize me. I met their clerical insults with respectful silence. I just kept on opening new parishes and urging people to come back to Church. In a relatively short time, the Masses were filled with worshipers.

A pro-communist newspaper wrote, "Cardinal Roncalli uses his sovereignty moderately and tactfully, but this does not change the fact that he is an absolute monarch. There is no doubt, however, that he is an open-minded and tolerant monarch."

In February 1957 there was a meeting of the thirty-second Congress of the Socialist Party of Italy. I had notices plastered on walls all over Venice, which said: "I welcome the exceptional significance of this event, which is so important for the future of our country. I should like to believe that the decisive motive for your assembly is to understand contemporary conditions and to devote yourselves to doing everything possible to improve living conditions and social well-being."

An anxious journalist questioned my welcoming such a group. I replied, "Don't be disturbed by my initiative. One day all those people I addressed will come to church again, too."[10]

I suppose you could say my peace strategy was proclamation rather than confrontation. I have been blessed with the gift of patience and the long-range view and have learned from experience that the positive preaching and witnessing of Christ, coupled with respectful treatment of those with whom I disagreed, generally did the most good.

To make this work, you must learn how to resist the first impulses to anger and retaliation which naturally surface when faced with hostile or negative behavior. Always take a longer view beyond this momentary jolt. The occasion has potential for healing, unity and peace, even if not apparent to you. Be quick to hear, slow to speak and definitely slow to anger. Think to yourself that peace is a far greater achievement than the momentary satisfaction of putting the other person down, or standing for your own wounded dignity.

Recall that God has put into every human heart a basic drive to peace, even if it has been shadowed by hostility, hatred and antagonism. You can trust that this gift of the potential for peace lies hidden in that person or group, even if long crusted over by biases, misunderstandings or other self-defeating treatment.

My three decades in the Church's diplomatic corps placed me in numerous touchy situations, the suspicions of the Orthodox Church of Catholics in Bulgaria, the well-remembered history of the Crusades by the Moslems in Turkey, the anger of the French government about bishops who collaborated with the Nazis. I gained plenty of practice in peacemaking, ecumenical sensitivity, interfaith skills and diplomacy.

I learned that peacemaking was possible, and it did far more good than perpetuating rigid barriers between the Church and these constituencies. I never yielded my Catholic beliefs and convictions in this process of peacemaking; in fact it was exactly my faith that strengthened me in this task. This may help you to see why I was so well prepared for the ecumenical movement that obtained such a positive role in the council. And it made possible my outreach to Krushchev at a critical moment in world history.

You will never regret being a peacemaker. You won't find it easy. Reconciling adversaries, whether religious or political or familial, is a practical application of the reconciling work of Jesus on the cross.

3. Pray for peace.

Wars come to an end, but the effort to maintain peace must never stop. From the perspective of faith, we can never let up praying for peace. The achievement of peace is more than a matter of diplomatic skills, psychological insight or being a natural-born bargainer. The wisdom of our Catholic people makes this evident in times of war, for they crowd the churches and implore God for peace. They instinctively know that this dream and goal is above all a gift from God.

> So magnificent, so exalted is this aim that human resources alone, even though inspired by the most praiseworthy good will, cannot hope to achieve it. God Himself must come to man's aid with his Heavenly assistance, if human society is to bear the closest possible resemblance to the kingdom of God.[11]

My prayers for peace motivated me to work for peace. God's grace moved me to write an encyclical which I hoped would help the world's nations to pursue by all means possible the dream and ideal of peace. I signed the first five copies of *Pacem in Terris* on Tuesday of Holy Week in 1963 in my private library before television lights. I wore a stole to indicate that this was a religious event. It even became an artistic occasion, for this encyclical was the only one ever set to music—by the French composer Darius Milhaud.

Published as it was during the season of the Church's celebration of the paschal mystery, the encyclical reflected the liturgical teachings about the ultimate source of peace:

> The very order of things, therefore, demands that during this sacred season we pray earnestly to Him who by His bitter passion and death washed away men's sins, which are the fountainhead of discord, misery and inequality; to Him who shed His blood to reconcile the human race to the heavenly Father, and bestowed the gifts of peace. "For he is our peace, who hath made both one.... And coming, He preached peace to you that were afar off; and to them that were nigh."
>
> The sacred liturgy of these days re-echoes the

> same message: "Our Lord Jesus Christ, after his resurrection, stood in the midst of His disciples and said: Peace be upon you, alleluia. The disciples rejoiced when they saw the Lord." It is Christ, therefore, who brought us peace; Christ bequeathed it to us: "Peace I leave with you: my peace I give to you: not as the world gives do I give unto you."
>
> Let us, then, pray with all fervor for this peace which our divine Redeemer came to bring us. May He banish from the souls of men whatever might endanger peace. May He transform all men into witnesses of truth, justice and brotherly love. May He illumine with His light the minds of rulers, so that, besides caring for the proper material welfare of their peoples, they may also guarantee them the fairest gift of peace.[12]

My long years of meditation on the "golden book"—*The Imitation of Christ*, bore into my bones the conviction that faith and prayer are the starting points for peace. I have heard politicians speak of peace through strength, by which they normally meant military might. But my own view of strength is spiritual power which unlocks the creativity needed to find ways to help people achieve peace in the world.

> [B]e peaceful yourself, and you will be able to bring peace to others....
>
> You readily excuse and explain your own doings, but you will not accept the explanations of others. It would be more just to accuse yourself, and to excuse your fellows. If you wish others to bear with you, you must bear with them. See how far you are from true charity and humility, which feels no anger nor indignation towards any save self. It is no great matter to associate with the good and gentle, for this is naturally pleasant to everyone. All men are glad to live at peace, and prefer those who are of their own

way of thinking. But to be able to live at peace among hard, obstinate, and undisciplined people and those who oppose us, is a great grace, and a most commendable and manly achievement.[13]

I have never lost my faith in the possibilities of peace, both for myself and for the world. God's picture of the peaceable kingdom in Isaiah 11:3-9 is a dream that never ceases to inspire me with hope. I do believe the wolf can lie down with the lamb. I am convinced that the cow and the bear can feed together. I have no doubt a little child shall lead them, that child who is the Son of God and Messiah, at whose birth angels filled the skies with the harmonies of peace. Without a vision, people would perish.

If life were only facts, this confidence would be hard for me. But life is mystery and possibility which stretches my heart far beyond facts, even while realistically facing them. Peace is the persuasive possibility that should enchant us all.

For Reflection

1. Bring order to your inner life.

Saint Jane Frances de Chantal once spoke to her sisters about a martyrdom of the spirit that is as powerful as martyrdom of the body. A sister asked what it was like.

> Yield yourself fully to God, and you will find out! Divine love takes its sword to the hidden recesses of our inmost soul and divides us from ourselves.[14]

Another sister wondered how long this process would take.

> From the moment when we commit ourselves

> unreservedly to God, until our last breath. I am speaking, of course, of great-souled individuals who keep nothing back for themselves, but instead are faithful in love.... [T]he martyrs of love suffer infinitely more in remaining in this life so as to serve God, than if they died a thousand times over in testimony to their faith and love and fidelity.[15]

Love of God is the principal means of putting order and peace into our disordered souls. It is a continual martyrdom.

- *How convinced are you of this truth of faith? What must you do to enter this process?*
- *What are you keeping back for yourself that is blocking your love for Christ?*

2. Be a peacemaker.

The government of Florence sent Catherine of Siena to Avignon to negotiate a peace between it and the papacy. She used the opportunity to urge the Pope to bring the papacy back to Rome. She was not shy in addressing Gregory XI on behalf of peace.

> Be a man Father! Arise! Do not be negligent!... Begin the reform of the Church through appointing worthy priests. Make peace in Italy, not by arms, but by pardon and mercy. Return to Rome, not with swords and soldiers, but with the Cross and the Blessed Lamb. O Father! Peace, for the love of God.[16]

- *How do you go about making peace at home in your family and with your friends, when this is needed?*
- *What do you find are the best ways to make peace among those you know?*
- *What public efforts have you made toward world peace?*

3. Pray for peace.

The Prayer of Saint Francis is one of the most beloved prayers in the world. Its opening line sets the theme of peace, "Lord, make me an instrument of your peace." Each line of the prayer teaches a way to become a peacemaker.

- *Review the words of Saint Francis' prayer and notice which verses touch your heart the most.*
- *Look at the words of the hymn, "Let There Be Peace on Earth and Let It Begin With Me." Which lines help you best to pray for peace?*
- *What other peace prayers do you use?*

Closing Prayer

Dear Jesus, when you were on earth you prayed the psalms. Possibly on your journey to Jerusalem as a lad of twelve you sang the words of Psalm 122. As you entered the gates of the holy city, you would have sung with the pilgrims:

> Pray for the peace of Jerusalem:
> May they prosper who love you.
> Peace be within your walls
> and security within your towers.[17]

Enable us to pray and work for peace as you did. Show us that the journey to peace begins within our souls, then in our families, among our friends and in our neighborhood—and finally in our nation and the world itself. Like the angels, may we become messengers of peace.

Notes

[1] Adapted from *I Will Be Called John*, pp. 306-310.

[2] Wisdom 7:25-26, 29-30; 8:2, *NRSV*.

[3] *Time,* January 4, 1962, p. 54.

[4] *Journal of a Soul*, p. 88.

[5] *Pope John XXIII*, p. 82.

[6] 1 Thessalonians 4:3-4, 7-8, *NRSV*.

[7] Ian Kerr, *Newman On Being a Christian* (London: HarperCollins Publishers Limited, 1990), pp. 123-124; 146.

[8] Luke 24:32, *NRSV*.

[9] *Journal of a Soul*, p. 127.

[10] Adapted from *A Pope Laughs*, pp. 104-105.

[11] *Pacem in Terris*, 168.

[12] Ibid., 169-171.

[13] *Imitation of Christ*, p. 70-71.

[14] Memoirs of Jane Frances de Chantal quoted in *Liturgy of the Hours*, vol. 1, pp. 1240-1241.

[15] Ibid.

[16] *Saints Are People*, p. 73.

[17] Psalm 122:6-7, *NRSV*.

Day Seven

My Bags Are Packed

Coming Together in the Spirit

"This bed is an altar. The altar demands a victim. I am ready."

When I entered my sixtieth year I said to myself, "I am growing old. I must prepare for death. I must simplify my life." But it was not until I turned eighty that I realized my end was approaching. I noticed in my body the beginning of real trouble that was natural for an old man. I tried to bear it patiently and put aside my fear that it would get worse.

The doctors told me I have a gastropathic condition. I laughed aloud and said, "That is because I am pope. Otherwise you would call it a stomach ache." The Roman newspapers are reporting that I am at death's door. I said to a friend, "Tell them the pope still lives. And there is no reason to bury him before he dies."[1]

Dr. Piero Mazzoni has moved into the Apostolic palace to watch over me and give me the attention I will need. He came just in time. Three days after his arrival, I suffered a massive intestinal hemorrhage and was in severe pain. He administered blood thinners, blood plasma and morphine. By daylight my bleeding had subsided. Terribly weakened, I had to cancel my Wednesday audience.

Under Dr. Mazzoni's loving care and a good deal of rest, I rallied finally. Though I was not strong enough to give any Wednesday audiences, I determined to give a blessing from my window. The council fathers adjourned their sessions to join the crowd which had filled St. Peter's Square. When I appeared at the fourth-floor window, a joyful burst of horns and cheers swept up toward me. Moved by their affection, I wept. "My children, as you see, Providence is with us. From day to day there is progress...*piano, piano* [slowly], sickness, then convalescence. And your presence gives us joy and strength and vigor."[2]

My bags were packed. I was ready to go. But I had some unfinished business. There were urgent matters that claimed my attention such as getting the council off to a good start, writing *Pacem in Terris* and saying good-bye to my family and friends.

I was at a point where I could summarize some of the things my life experience had taught me. In a meeting with Cardinal Amleto Cigognani I said:

> Today more than ever, certainly more than in previous centuries, we are called to serve man as such, and not merely Catholics; to defend above all and everywhere the rights of the human person, and not merely those of the Catholic Church. Today's world, the needs made plain in the last fifty years, and a deeper understanding of doctrine have brought us to a new situation, as I said in my opening speech to the Council. It is not that the Gospel has changed: it is that we have begun to understand it better. Those who have lived as long as I have were faced with new tasks in the social order at the start of the century; those who, like me, were twenty years in the East and eight years in France, were enabled to compare different cultures and

> traditions, and know that the moment has come to discern the signs of the times, to seize the opportunity and to look far ahead.[3]

Defining Our Thematic Context

Wise People Ponder Eternity

As we come to the final day of our retreat, let me review the steps toward wisdom which we have taken: (1) Begin with love of God, others and self. (2) Adopt voluntary simplicity. (3) Calm down your inner soul. (4) Embrace the joy of humility. (5) Love the Church. (6) Ask Jesus to make you an instrument of his peace.

On this seventh day I ask you to contemplate wisdom as an insight into eternity. God created the biblical sabbath so we should have time to pray and play. To pray means to worship God, to thank him for the gifts of life, family and the means to sustain them. Prayer, by its nature turns our attention to eternity, where God lives in glory and calls us to our final destiny. Even the "play" and relaxation of the sabbath—for us, the Christian Sunday—is an ingenious way of stopping the clock, of removing ourselves from the toils of time, and, in a sense, rehearsing for eternity.

One of the wisest men who ever lived was Saint Thomas Aquinas. When asked what he thought was the meaning of wisdom, he said it is the outcome of meditating on our ultimate origin and destiny and applying the insights to practical daily living. When thinking of our origins, we tend to settle for our family background, our ethnic ancestry and our present cultural and political citizenship. Of course, this is part of the picture. I have often talked to you about my life in Sotto il Monte and my family influences. But you and I must dig deeper, into our very roots in eternity. When our parents conceived us, God was there to give us a soul. God is the ultimate author of our lives.

Thomas taught that wise people also ponder their destiny. When I grew very ill, I thought of doctors and medicine and unfinished business. And that was right. But I also realized that my destiny in eternity demanded my attention. Wisdom pierces through the secondary events of time to deal with the most basic questions of life: Where did I come from? Where am I going?

Yesterday, the sixth day of our retreat, I asked you to review the role of peacemaking, an essential feature of wisdom. I urged you to: (1) Bring order to your inner life. (2) Be a peacemaker. (3) Pray for peace. Now, as I ask you to focus on the infinite expanse of eternity, would you pray with me?

Opening Prayer

Eternal Father, strong to save,
the heights of the mountains and the depths of the sea
image for us the vastness of eternity. But...
nature's symbols pale before our experience of love.
When we say love is stronger than death,
we affirm eternity as the fulfillment
of our deepest longings,
not just eternity in contrast to time,
but love unfulfilled to love completely satisfied.

You revealed this when you said to Jesus,
"Beloved Son."
And when Jesus smiled at you and said,
"Abba, Father."
And when the Spirit came to show us that your love

was so astonishing that it is the best name
we have for your eternal communion with each other.

The saints tell us we should prepare for death,
and so we should—
but not death as a mysterious and tragic end,
rather death as the opportunity for eternity.
Preparing to die means little
if it does not mean preparing for absolute love
for communion with you, our origin and destiny.

Sing for us the music of our homeland,
melodies that melt all our resistance
to be with you,
tunes that turn us toward our heavenly goal,
harmonies that hold us tightly fixed on you,
songs of love that charm away our fears,
sounds of eternal silence
more rapturous than all earth's noise.

RETREAT SESSION SEVEN

The Resurrection of the Body

Every time we recite the creed we restate our faith in the resurrection of the body. Christianity moved the sabbath from Saturday to Sunday, a day of joy which celebrates the resurrection of Jesus. The resurrection of Christ's body is a foretaste of our own and a confirmation of our eternal destiny.

The summit of the liturgical year climaxes with Easter, Christ's triumph over death, eternity's victory over time. When our eyes of faith are fixed on Easter, then everything else makes sacred sense. The Easter sun shines back on history and lights up the landscape of the story of salvation. Its brilliant rays shine forward into our own days and up to the final coming of Jesus which will be the last act in the divine plan of salvation.

Of course, all the mysteries of Christ's life form an indivisible unity—incarnation, baptism, transfiguration, preaching, miracles, and passion and death. But it is his resurrection that helps us look back and behold with faith how that all fits together. I draw your attention to the emphasis on the resurrection of the body. Easter is not just about the immortality of the soul but also about the participation of the body in eternal life. It is perhaps this aspect of the mystery that more effectively reminds us of eternal life than the durability of our souls, though both achieve the same goal.

When Saint Paul preached in Corinth he encountered a culture that was preoccupied with the body both as an instrument of sexuality and a disciplined force for the Isthmian games, sports events that attracted widespread attention. They could not help but be interested in Paul's proclamation of Christ's resurrection from the dead. They asked him, "How are the dead raised? With what kind of body will they come?" Paul answered, "What you sow does not come to life unless it dies. And as for what you sow, you do not sow the body that is to be, but a bare seed, perhaps of wheat or some other grain.... So it is with the resurrection of the dead. What is sown is perishable, what is raised is imperishable."[4]

If you are a gardener or a farmer, this image will appeal to you. Hold an acorn in your hand. Now look at an oak tree. They don't look one bit alike, yet they are intrinsically related. The acorn is planted in the death of the earth, then rises to become a majestic tree. It will be the same with our bodies, planted in the grave, but due to rise one day by God's power and participate in eternal life. So you see it was through the mystery of the body that Paul was able to explain what the resurrection was about and bring them to a sense of future life in eternity.

In your own times, my successor, Pope John Paul II has explored the religious meaning of the body. His Wednesday audiences for a period of two years were devoted to an explanation of the first chapters of the Book of Genesis. He dwelt at great length on the creation of the body and its use in revealing to us our identity as images of God as well as a sign of our humanity, masculinity and femininity. He did this as preoccupation with the body was growing in modern society. The doctrine of the resurrection of our bodies confirms our body's religious meaning as well as its essential connection to our humanity.

In my reflections on the mysteries of the rosary, I had this to say about the first glorious mystery, the resurrection of Jesus.

> The Resurrection marks the greatest victory of Christ, and likewise the assurance of victory for the holy Catholic Church, beyond all the adversities and persecutions of past yesterdays and tomorrow's future. "Christ conquers, reigns and rules." We do well to remember that the first appearance of the risen Christ was to the pious women, who were near to him during his humble life, who had accompanied him in his sufferings as far as Calvary, and stayed with him there.
>
> In the splendour of this mystery we see with the eyes of faith, as living and united with the risen Jesus, the souls who were most dear to us, the souls of those who lived with us and whose sufferings we shared. How vividly the memory of our dead rises in our hearts in the light of the Resurrection of Christ!

> We remember and pray for them in the very sacrifice of our crucified and risen Lord, and they still share the best part of our life which is prayer and Jesus.
>
> The Eastern liturgy wisely concludes the funeral rite with the "Alleluia!" for all the dead. While we implore the light of eternal habitations for our dead, at the same time our thoughts turn to the resurrection which awaits our mortal remains: *Et exspecto resurrectionem mortuorum* ["I expect the resurrection of the dead."]. Learning to wait, trusting always to the precious promise of which the Resurrection of Jesus gives us a sure pledge—this is a foretaste of heaven.[5]

We have opened six doors to the mystery of wisdom: love, simplicity, tranquility, humility, love for the Church and peacemaking. Now let us turn to the seventh clue to wisdom's meaning, eternity.

1. Love life.

During one of my audiences, I said, "We will pray for you, for your families. And do you also pray for your Pope. For, to be frank, permit me to tell you that I wish to live a long time. I love life."[6]

Allow me to have a little dialogue with you on this point. What are you thinking?

Reader: How can you say I should love life here and yet long for eternity as well?

John: It looks like a contradiction to you.

Reader: Did not Jesus say we should lose our life in order to gain it? And what about Christ telling us to lose the self, deny the self? That does not sound like loving life.

John: You think I am sending you a mixed message?

Reader: The central image in every Church is the crucifix.

Jesus died to this life. And look at all the times he spoke of eternal life, especially in such attractive images, like a wedding banquet. Jesus tried to get us to let go of this life and love eternal life.

John: But Jesus willed to live a human life, to experience what it was like from our viewpoint. He thought with a human mind, loved with a human heart and worked with a human body. He seemed to cherish and enjoy human life.

Reader: Jesus only took on human life so that we could achieve divine life.

John: Does that mean that he had little regard for human life? That he had little respect for the humanity he both created and assumed? He lived a human life for thirty-three years. He seemed to enjoy it. He attended weddings, mourned at funerals, feasted at dinner parties—even hosted his own with the miracle of the loaves.

Reader: He was born in poverty, had no place to lay his head, met hatred, misunderstanding, rejection and failure. Most of his experience of human life was not all that pleasant.

John: Did not Jesus see the potential for joy in life? Why else did he give sight to the blind, open the ears of the deaf, help the mute to speak and raise the dead from the grave? He even made sure that the poor had the Good News preached to them.

Reader: Exactly my point. The Good News he preached to them was the Kingdom of Heaven, future life, eternal life—not a love of this life.

John: Is human life a gift from God?

Reader: Yes.

John: Surely we should love and reverence God's gifts.

Reader: Of course.

John: It seems to me that we are faced here with a both-and, not an either-or.

Reader: What do you mean?

John: Well, you agree with me that human life is God's gift and should be loved. And I agree with you that eternal life is also God's gift and should be loved and longed for.

Reader: All right, where does that lead us?

John: From the viewpoint of faith, this tells us that loving life here does not necessarily mean excluding a passion for life hereafter.

Reader: I'm not sure I follow you.

John: Jesus did not separate the future life from this one into watertight compartments. In his own being he combined the divine and the human into a harmonious unity. Jesus, the baby born of Mary, was also the Son of God.

Reader: So in Jesus there was no wall of separation of the human and the divine, of human and divine life.

John: They were integrated into one person. Read again his dialogue with the religious leaders in John, Chapter 6. When Jesus speaks about the Bread of Life, he says it will give us eternal life right now and resurrection of the body on the last day (John 6:54).

Reader: I'm beginning to see your line of thought. In the Eucharist, as in all the sacraments, I already possess a beginning of the eternal life that lies ahead for me after death.

John: Now carry that a step further. That divine, eternal life—also called grace—helps your human life to achieve its full potential.

Reader: Is that what Saint Irenaeus meant when he said, "The glory of God is a man fully alive"?

John: Eternal life working on our human life here makes our humanity become what it was meant to be. Eternal life provides what your modern self-fulfillment movements hope to achieve. Only it works better because the author of human life, who knows what we are meant to be, is lovingly working within us.

Reader: So your love of life here always includes love of eternal life....

John: Which is present here by the work of the Holy Spirit....

Reader: Making the best sense of the maxim: "Become all that you can be."

John: I couldn't have said it better.

2. Don't be afraid of Sister Death.

> It is an indisputable truth that all of us one day will receive a visit from our Sister Death, as St. Francis of Assisi called her. She sometimes presents herself in a sudden and unexpected manner. But we shall remain tranquil, or better undisturbed, if our tree has known how to yield its fruits. He who has worked well, departs when the day has ended.[7]

John: Would you like to continue our conversation?

Reader: I thought I heard you say earlier that we should dwell more on the truth of eternity than on the subject of death.

John: I believe that is more fruitful.

Reader: But now you make me look at Sister Death.

John: Is it unpleasant for you?

Reader: I prefer thinking of life.

John: In a retreat I made over twenty years ago, I wrote these words: "I await the arrival of Sister Death calmly and gladly. I shall welcome her in a manner that is in keeping with which it shall please the Lord to surround her."

Reader: Why was that important for you?

John: Death should never be trivialized or ignored. Wars and the Holocaust have caused over one hundred million violent deaths in the twentieth century. When killing is commonplace, life is cheapened.

Reader: Does attention to the role of death have an effect on the way we live?

John: Where there is reverence for life, then death assumes its Christian meaning as a transition to eternal life. When death is seen as our Sister, then it becomes the midwife helping us to be born into eternal life.

Reader: Would you say that death is life's most important event?

John: After being born, death is the one event we all share together, rich and poor, strong and weak, virtuous and vicious. Death is a significant moment for each of us. But more important than death is God's love which saves us in baptism, the other sacraments and the life-giving power of the indwelling of the Holy Spirit. With this divine Love, we conquer death, cease to fear it and welcome it as our Sister.

Reader: I live in a culture which has an increasing incidence of violent deaths—and the moral tragedy of one million abortions a year. Yet my culture adores youth, or at least looking young. Between diets and cosmetic surgery many people pursue the illusion that age isn't affecting them.

John: In other words, death bothers them, even if they do not speak about it.

Reader: This has been called a massive denial of death.

John: Which also means denying the next life. Once that happens, then eternal life has no effect on human life here.

Reader: It's like the children's game, "Let's pretend."

John: Yet you tell me your generation prides itself on being honest and open. "Brutally frank," as you often say.

Reader: Except on the question of dying. Naturally, it cannot be ignored when one has a fatal disease, or is on life support systems or in the intensive care wards of hospitals.

John: But by then a lifetime of denial takes its toll.

Reader: Yes, it would be better had we welcomed Sister Death while we were yet healthy. She might look more welcoming to us rather than like a fearsome visitor.

John: Properly understood she will seem less like a closed door, a dead end, and more like a clean window pane, through which we get hints of the light of future glory.

Reader: That's what you've been trying to tell me all along.

John: I had to grow in faith just like you. I have been blessed with a family full of faith and with a multitude of graces which have shaped my life and sharpened my vision. I owe it all to God.

Reader: You've made me feel more at home with Sister Death.

John: Good! She will share with you her secrets of wisdom that will comfort you—not frighten you.

3. Hunger for eternal life.

> "I am wholly ready to go where the Lord calls me. I desire to be dissolved and to be with Christ." [To] Msgr. Rocca: "I thank you for all the services that you have rendered me. We shall continue to love each other in heaven."[8]

John: I'm enjoying our dialogue. I hope you feel the same way.

Reader: It helps me understand your teaching, and perhaps you can appreciate what difficulties I have.

John: Earlier, you mentioned that you are attracted to the call to eternal life.

Reader: When you ask me to hunger for it I can tell you that means a lot to me.

John: It attracts you.

Reader: When I was a teenager I felt immortal. I could not imagine death touching me. I liked that feeling of immortality even though it was an illusion in the sense I had it then. I did not connect it with God. I thought I was the source of my own forever-ness.

John: Time has changed you?

Reader: Going through the life stages of young adulthood and my middle years, with all the problems and disappointments made me realize my limits.

John: Nonetheless, you feel a longing for the infinite.

Reader: I never let go of my faith. I drifted from the Church for a while, but returned after my marriage and the birth of our children.

John: The life cycle and its responsibilities teaches its own lessons.

Reader: My idealism suffered some blows along the way but remained basically intact. I moved from being the godlike youth to a humbler position before the real God.

John: That's a rewarding development.

Reader: In a culture where everything is relative, where so many of my friends are divorced, I feel the need to belong to a God whose love for me is absolute.

John: And One who will offer you eternal life right now.

Reader: That's the most appealing of his promises.

John: God was always offering you the option for love.

Reader: It took me a while to notice it. When I found myself once again drawn to prayer, I realized that God was quietly leading me back to himself. There was no other explanation.

John: God is a persistent lover. Rejection and refusal by us only increase his desire to have us accept his love.

Reader: That made me feel guilty at first, thinking of how often I had refused God's love. Then I realized God seeks a hundred ways to break through my resistance to his love. I shed my guilt and was overcome by gratitude.

John: You would find a kindred soul in Saint Augustine. He described God shouting at him and piercing his spiritual deafness.

Reader: That's just what happened to me. Oddly I never thought I was shutting God out of my life.

John: Does your longing for eternal life make your fear of death less acute?

Reader: Much less, though I still shiver at the thought of it.

John: Jesus shuddered at the presence of death when he approached the tomb of Lazarus. At Gethsemane, the thought of death caused sweat like drops of blood to flow from his head. We welcome Sister Death, but our natural resistance, our instinct for self-preservation pulls us the other way.

Reader: I'm gathering that's part of the process of coming to terms with death and looking beyond to eternal life.

John: In the end you can find peace and acceptance as you draw closer to our heavenly home.

Reader: I'll stay in training now, hungering for eternal life, so I won't be playing catch-up at the end.

John: That is a grace and a blessing for which you will praise and thank God with a full heart. You know my bags are packed. I'm ready to go. This blessed assurance will be yours as well.

For Reflection

1. Love life.

Pope John told Dr. Mazzoni that he would like to meet his family. The doctor, his wife and two daughters came on the following Sunday. "He was so kind, so *interested* in them. He talked to them for half an hour. Later, I asked my younger daughter who was then eight, what she thought of the pope. She said he looked like an ordinary priest, and I could tell she was disappointed. But when she is older and can understand such a thing, I will explain to her that that was Pope John's glory, that he was just an ordinary priest—who took Christianity seriously."[9]

- *What are three examples from Pope John's story that show you how much he loved life? How has he helped you to love life?*
- *Why is his interest in people—such as Dr. Mazzoni's family—an example of love for life?*
- *Why is it important to love human life?*

2. Don't be afraid of Sister Death.

> I'm not aware of having offended anyone, but if I have I beg their forgiveness; and if you know anyone who has not been edified by my attitudes or actions, ask them to have compassion on me and to forgive me. In this last hour I feel calm and sure that my Lord, in his mercy, will not reject me.... My time on earth is drawing to a close. But Christ lives on and the Church continues his work. Souls, souls.[10]

- *How can you tell whether you are coming to terms with death? Why should you try?*
- *What do you think helped Pope John welcome Sister Death?*
- *How did Pope John's appreciation of the role of death in the midst of life give him wisdom? What will you do to grow in wisdom?*

3. Hunger for eternal life.

> What grace, sweetness and solemnity in the scene of Mary's "falling asleep," as the Christans of the East

imagine it! She is lying in the serene sleep of death; Jesus stands beside her, and clasps her soul, as if it were a tiny child, to his heart, to indicate the miracle of her immediate resurrection and glorification.

The Christians of the West, raising their eyes and hearts to heaven, choose to portray Mary borne body and soul to the eternal kingdom. The greatest artists saw her thus, incomparable in her divine beauty. Oh let us too go with her, borne aloft by her escort of angels.[11]

- *How can meditation on the mystery of Mary's glorious assumption into heaven draw you to develop a longing for eternal life?*
- *Why is your faith in the resurrection of your body an important part of your desire for eternal life? What does this teaching say about how to treat your body in this life?*
- *Truly wise people view their lives in terms of their origin in God and their destiny with God in eternal life. What will you do to embark on this path of wisdom?*

Closing Prayer

Wise Father, your Son is incarnate wisdom and the Holy Spirit imparts to us the gift of wisdom. Blessed Mary is the seat of wisdom. And all the saints arrived at holiness, led by the Spirit of wisdom. We find ourselves distracted by the world and all too seldom drawn to divine wisdom.

In this retreat we have meditated on the seven pillars of wisdom: love, simplicity, inner calm, humility, love for the Church, peacemaking, eternity. These are like the seven lampstands of the Book of Revelation. They light our way to Jesus Christ, incarnate wisdom.

We know that we walk by faith and not by sight. Help then, O Lord, our unbelief and make our faith abound. May our first waking thoughts be directed to you and our closing thoughts at night be fixed on you. Direct all our thoughts, words and deeds of every day to do your will. What could be a surer path to wisdom than this plan?

We thank you for the graces of this retreat and believe this has been another fruitful step on our journey to you in eternal glory. Stay with us, Lord, at every moment. This we ask through Jesus Christ, your Son and through the Holy Spirit, forever and ever. Amen.

Notes

[1] Adapted from *I Will Be Called John*, p. 313.

[2] Ibid., p. 314.

[3] *Pope John XXIII*, pp. 498-499.

[4] 1 Corinthians 15:35-37; 42, *NRSV*.

[5] *Journal of a Soul*, pp. 370-371.

[6] *A Pope Laughs*, p. 183.

[7] Ibid., p. 184.

[8] Ibid., p. 187.

[9] Adapted from *I Will Be Called John*, p. 317.

[10] *Pope John XXIII*, p. 502.

[11] *Journal of a Soul*, p. 372.

One More Word From Pope John XXIII

My dear sisters and brothers, I, Pope John XXIII, thank you for joining me in this retreat where we have reflected on seven gateways to wisdom. Together we have looked at the power of love, the pleasures of the simple life, the grace of inner peace, the secret joys of humility, the benefits of loving the Church, the persistent call to make peace and the beneficial impact of longing for eternity.

People have called me a wise man. If that be so, I can tell you it took a long time and required the Holy Spirit to work strenuously on my mind, heart and body. Whatever wisdom I have is the result of God's amazing grace. I did not present myself to you as a model. I wanted you to see Jesus acting in me. If I used stories from my life, that was not to fix your attention on me but only to show you how extraordinary is the power of Christ in my life.

Now you continue on your faith journey. I give you my blessing, even as I blessed multitudes in my lifetime. And I shall pray for you. I did not cease to be a shepherd just because I have left this earth. I love you with all my paternal and priestly heart. Take my blessing and my love and be on your way.

Walk joyfully in the Lord, singing psalms of praise. Little by little people will notice wisdom in your eyes, flowing from faith in your heart. They will say, "How did this happen?" And you may reply, "I think of love, simplicity...." And the presence of Jesus will slowly form in them.

Deepening Your Acquaintance

To learn more about Pope John XXIII, consider these resources:

Elliott, Lawrence. *I Will Be Called John: A Biography of Pope John XXIII*. New York: Reader's Digest Press, E.P. Dutton and Company, Inc., 1973.

Hebblethwaite, Peter. *Pope John XXIII: Shepherd of the Modern World*. Garden City, N.Y.: Doubleday & Company, 1985.

Kaiser, Robert Blair. *Pope, Council and World: The Story of Vatican II*. New York: Macmillan, 1963.

Klinger, Kurt. *A Pope Laughs: Stories of John XXIII*, trans. from the German by Sally McDevitt Cunneen. Chicago: Holt, Rinehart & Winston, 1964.

Pope John XXIII. *Journal of a Soul*, trans. Dorothy White. New York: McGraw-Hill Book Company, 1965.

_____. *Letters to His Family*, trans. Dorothy White. New York: McGraw-Hill Book Company, 1969.

Trevor, Meriol. *Pope John*. New York: Doubleday & Company, 1967.

Wit and Wisdom of Good Pope John, collected by Henri Fesquet, trans. Salvator Attanasio. New York: P.J. Kenedy & Sons, 1964.